THE ORIGIN OF MATHEMATICS

D1590651

V. Lakshmikantham
and
S. Leela

University Press of America, ® Inc.
Lanham • New York • Oxford

Copyright © 2000 by
University Press of America
4720 Boston Way
Lanham, Maryland 20706

12 Hid's Copse Rd.
Cumnor Hill, Oxford OX2 9JJ

Library of Congress Cataloging-in-Publication Data

Lakshmikantham, V.
The origin of mathematics / V. Lakshmikantham and S. Leela.
p. cm.
Includes bibliographical references and index.
1. Mathematics—India History. 2. Mathematics, Ancient.
I. Leela, S. II. Title.
QA27.I4 L34 2000 510'.934—dc21 00-032520 CIP

ISBN 0-7618-1736-0 (cloth: alk. ppr.)
ISBN 0-7618-1737-9 (pbk: alk. ppr.)

⊖™The paper used in this publication meets the minimum
requirements of American National Standard for Information
Sciences—Permanence of Paper for Printed Library Materials,
ANSI Z39.48—1984

Contents

List of Figures

List of Tables

Preface

From the late eighteenth century, the Western scholarship on India was influenced by the prevalent European historical and philosophical methodologies as well as the colonial interests. Two speculative theories were invented which are responsible for doing a great injustice to India's position in the world. One of them is that Aryans did not originate from India but invaded from elsewhere, which is known as the theory of Aryan invasion of India. The other theory is that the first ages of the Hindus are chiefly mythological and thus the historical age of India cannot be carried further back to 2000 years before Christ. On the basis of this, the chronology of ancient India was reduced arbitrarily by more than 1200 years by misidentifying Chandragupta Maurya (1534-1500 B.C.) with Chandragupta (327-320 B.C.) of Gupta dynasty as a contemporary of Alexander the Great. Because of these two invented theories, which are still in standard books, the times of many prominent figures, including ancient mathematicians, have been pushed forward into the Christian Era. Moreover, the age of Rig Veda was also fixed as 1200 B.C. which was supposed to have written by the invading Aryans who were nomads.

All these Eurocentric inventions have led to the persistent habit of looking outside of India for the origin of everything. This has its root in one fixed idea that everything really great in ancient India has been introduced by foreigners.

With this background, let us consider the origin of mathematics. In 1875, G. Thibaut translated a large portion of the Sulvasutras, which are the sacred books for the design and construction of Vedic alters. They show that ancient Indian priests possessed significant mathematical knowledge.   Thibaut did not formulate the clear conclusion that Greeks were not the inventors of geometry but it was Indians. The Greek scholars, however, saw that this was the message in Thibaut's paper. They did not like it. The question was, if Indians invented plane geometry, what was to become of "Greek genius?" All the refutations were mere haughty dismissals.

Realizing the importance of Thibaut's work, M. Cantor began a comparative study of Greek and Indian mathematics. Assigning 100 B.C. as the date of Sulvasutras, Cantor claimed that Indians were the students of Greeks in geometry. He eventually renounced this view but still insisted that Pythagorus got his geometry from Egypt and not from India. The damage was done anyway and the Sulvasutras have never taken the position in the history of mathematics that they richly deserve.   Therefore, the foregone conclusion that "the history of mathematics cannot with certainty be traced back to any school or period before that of Greeks" has continued.

In 1928, Neugebauer translated Babylonian mathematical texts which showed that the theorem of Pythagorus was known over one thousand years before. Again, not everyone was willing to change their belief of Greek genius. In fact, M.S. Mahoney, in 1934, asserted that he would rather invoke the "Greek miracle" than assume that Babylonian mathematics was the basis for developments and the vast promise of pre-Greek mathematics is, to a large extent, illusory. As recently as in 1975, S. Unguru used an amazing trick to show that "it is all an illusion. The modern mathematicians, turned historians, look at ancient mathematics through modern literal eyeglasses, and see things that are not there."

Around the same time, A. Seidenberg was investigating the question of the origin of mathematics.   In his paper, in 1978, he established that the Sulvasutras as the basis for the mathematics in Egypt, Babylonia, and Greece. This, Seidenberg accomplished by pure rationalization without challenging the existing speculative theories.

A number of new books have recently been written which challenge many imposed assumptions of Eurocentric historians by presenting abundant evidence, linguistic, literary, archaeological, anthropological, geological, and astronomical. These books call for thorough revision of the erroneous history textbooks used in schools and colleges worldwide, including those of India. These new investigations prove that there never was any Aryan invasion of India. The Sanskrit-speaking people known as Vedic Aryans diffused from Bharata Varsha (greater India) to every part of the world. The cradle of civilization is not in Greece, not even Sumeria in Mesopotamia, but the Sapta Sindhu in northwest India. Rig Veda was not composed in 1200 B.C. but was compiled before 3000 B.C. Rig Veda is certainly not a product of a primitive culture but it is a product of people enjoying the fruits of mature civilization based on age-old traditions. The modern period of India starts from 3138 B.C., the time of Mahabharata war. The famous Buddha lived during 1887 to 1807 B.C. The first well known mathematician and astronomer, Aryabhatta was born in 2765 B.C. and Sulvasutras were compiled well before that date. Bhaskaracharya's *Siddhanta Siromani*, which is a well known mathematical text was written in 486 A.D.

After describing in detail the prevailing theories on the history of mathematics, Struik inserts in his book, the following scholarly remark that "ancient India may still yield many more mathematical treasures. We now know, for instance, that the Gregory-Leibniz series for $\frac{\pi}{4}$ can be found in a Sanskrit manuscript ascribed to Nilakanta (1500 A.D.)." It is in this spirit we see the importance of our monograph. It's aim is to report the rediscovered latent treasures of ancient India that have been neglected and buried under the influence of Eurocentric historical indifference.

In Chapter 1, we summarize the prevailing theories on the history of mathematics adapting from Struik's popular book. Chapter 2 traces the developments of the origin of mathematics following Seidenberg, who describes how the scholars have been invoking the Greek miracle even when they encountered the truth which is otherwise. We shall examine in Chapter 3, the invented speculative theories that have propagated only the European view of the world history, turning the history of non-European cultures into a mere footnote. In particular, these invented theories have created a persistent habit of looking outside of India for the origin of everything. We shall also provide the list of recent scholars whose works dismiss the invented theories and furnish solid evidence.

In Chapter 4, chronological aspects are described which establish the correct chronological history of ancient India as well as the dates of some prominent figures and mathematicians. We start with the mathematical results of Sulvasutras of Baudhayana, Apastamba and Katyayana, in Chapter 5. We then successively present the contributions to mathematics of Aryabhatta, the father of scientific astronomy, and Bhaskara I, the earliest exponent of Aryabhatta's school of astronomy. We continue in Chapter 6 with Brahmagupta who played a crucial role in the history of ancient mathematics and astronomy. We then introduce Bhaskaracharya who is the most famous and popular among Indian mathematicians and astronomers. Mahavira, Ganesa and Nilakanta follow these great mathematicians with their own significant contribution.

Since all mathematicians of ancient India, including those who were in between the great proponents, were also astronomers, we devote Chapter 7 to describe the relevant astronomical aspects connected with mathematicians. Chapter 8 provides background data challenging the linear versions of the human past as well as that we know about the remote ancient period of Greece. We trace also the reasons for the decay of the glorious civilization and culture of ancient India relative to its great universities and traditional education. Finally, we list some of the important facts that need to be remembered.

We are well aware that changing one's cherished pet theories is rather difficult and quite threatening to scholars. Nonetheless, we have reported the true facts because compromising with falsehood is not considered as tolerance but as self-destruction.

Vedic scriptures say "that which remains invariant through the past, the present and the future, that alone is truth. That which changes is only illusion."

V. Lakshmikantham
S. Leela
July 1999

Chapter 1

Prevailing Theories

This chapter provides a compact summary of the origin of mathematics adapted from Struik's book which reflects the prevailing theories on the history of mathematics. This is a popular book which has been translated into several languages as well as revised and enlarged in the third edition. It lists the most important books on the history of mathematics that have been consulted and consequently, is treated as a standard text.

The first conceptions of number and form date back to time as far removed as the Old Stone Age, the Paleolithieum. In this period humans lived in caves, under conditions differing little from those of animals and their energies were directed towards the elementary process of collecting food wherever they could get it. They made weapons for hunting and fishing, developed a language to communicate with each other, and in the later Paleolithic ages enriched their lives with creative art forms, statuettes and paintings. Little progress was made in understanding numerical values and space relations until the transition occurred from the mere gathering of food to its actual production, from hunting and fishing to agriculture. With this fundamental change, we enter the New Stone Age, the Neolithieum, because the passive attitude of human beings turned into a revolutionary active one. This great event in the history of mankind occurred perhaps ten thousand years ago. Nomadic wandering in search of food came to an end and fishing and hunting were replaced by primitive farming. Gradually, elementary crafts such as pottery, carpentry, and weaving were developed. Bread was baked, beer was brewed, and in late Neolithic times, copper and bronze were smelted and inventions, such as the potters wheel and the wagon wheel were made.

During fifth, fourth and third millennium B.C., newer and more advanced forms of society evolved from the well-established Neolithic communities along the banks of great rivers in Africa and Asia, in subtropic or nearly subtropic regions. These rivers were Nile, the Tigris and Euphrates,the Indus and later the Ganges, the Huang Ho and later the Yang-tse. Oriental mathematics originated as a practical science in order to facilitate computation of the calender, administration of the harvest, organization of public works, and collection of taxes. The initial emphasis naturally was on practical arithmetic and mensuration. It always has been easy to differentiate between the arts and the script of the Egyptians, the Mesopotamians, the Chinese, and the Indians. Their general arithmetic-algebraic nature was very much alive.

It is difficult to date new discoveries in the East. The static character of its social structure has tended to preserve scientific lore throughout centuries or even millennia. Storages of scientific and technical knowledge have been destroyed by dynastic changes, wars or floods. There is a story that in 221 B.C., the Great Yellow Emperor Shih Huang-ti, had ordered all books of learning to be destroyed. Later many of them were rewritten by memory but such events make the dating of discoveries very difficult.

Another problem in dating oriental science is due to the material used for its preservation. The Mesopotamians used baked clay tablets, the Egyptians employed papyrus, the Chinese and the Indians used more perishable material. Thus our knowledge of oriental mathematics is very sketchy. For the pre-Hellenistic centuries, we are confined to Mesopotamian and Egyptian material. Most of our knowledge of Egyptian mathematics is derived from two mathematical papyri: The Papyrus Rhind and Moscow Papyrus. Mesopotamian mathematics reached a far higher level than Egyptian mathematics ever obtained. Older texts, dating from the latest Summerian period (2100 B.C.), show keen computational ability. Our present division of the hour into

60 minutes and 3600 seconds dates back to the Summerian, as does the division of the circle to 360 degrees. It is reasonable to suppose that both Hindus and Greeks made its acquaintance on the caravan routes through Babylon. We also know that the Muslim scholars described it as Indian invention. The Babylon tradition, however, may have influenced all later acceptance of the position system. The strong arithmetical-algebraic character of Babylonian mathematics is also apparent from its geometry but the geometrical form of the problem was only a way of presenting an algebraic question.

In all ancient oriental mathematics, nowhere do we find any attempt at what we call a *demonstration*. No arguments were presented, but only the prescription of certain rules: "Do such, do so."

The question of Greek, Chinese, and Babylonian influence determines profoundly the study of ancient Hindu mathematics. The Indian and Chinese scholars stress the great antiquity of their mathematics, but there are no mathematical texts in existence which can be positively dated to the pre-Christian era.

There exists the so-called Sulvasutras in India, parts of which date back to 500 B.C. or earlier. These contain mathematical rules used to construct alters for rituals. There is some knowledge of the Pythagorean theorem in specific cases, and there are a few curious approximations in terms of unit fractions, such as

$$\sqrt{2} = 1 + \tfrac{1}{3} + \tfrac{1}{3\times4} - \tfrac{1}{3\times3\times34} = 1.4142156,$$

and

$$\pi = 4\left(1 - \tfrac{1}{8} + \tfrac{1}{8\times29} - \tfrac{1}{8\times29\times6} + \tfrac{1}{8\times29\times6\times8}\right)^2 = 18\left(3 - 2\sqrt{2}\right).$$

The curious fact that these results of the Sulvasutras do not occur in later Hindu works shows that we cannot yet speak of that continuity of tradition in Hindu mathematics. However, it is entirely possible that new discoveries will lead to a complete re-evaluation of the relative merits of the different oriental forms of mathematics.

Enormous economical and political changes occurred around the Mediterranean basin during the last centuries of the second millennium. This turbulent atmosphere replaced the Bronze Age by the Age of Iron. Few details are known about this period of revolution, but we find that towards the end, perhaps around 900 B.C., the Minoan and Hittite empires had disappeared, the power of Egypt and Babylonia had greatly reduced, and new peoples had come into historical setting. No mathematical texts have come to us from this transition period.

The most outstanding of these new peoples were the Hebrews, the Assyrians, the Phoenicians, and the Greeks. The replacement of the Bronze Age by the Iron Age brought a change in warfare, stimulated trade, participation of common people in matters of economy and public interest, easy to learn script, and the introduction of coined money. The trading towns arose along the coast of Asia Minor and on the Greek mainland. During the seventh and sixth centuries B.C., the merchant class rose to ascendancy and the result was the rise of the Greek Polis, the self governing city state. This new social order created the new type of man, who could philosophize about his world. The absence of any well-established religion led many inhabitants of coastal towns into mysticism, but also stimulated its opposite, the growth of rationalism and the scientific outlook, abandoning the static outlook of the Orient.

Modern mathematics was born in this atmosphere of Ionian rationalism. The traditional father of Greek mathematics is the merchant, Thales of Milete, who visited Babylon and Egypt in the first half of the sixth century B.C. Even if his whole figure is legendary, it stands for something eminently real, since it symbolizes the circumstances under which the foundations of modern mathematics, science and philosophy were established. Although there is little doubt that the Greek merchants became acquainted with oriental mathematics, they soon discovered that the Orientals had left most of the rationalization undone.

Unfortunately there are no primary sources which can give us a picture of the early development of Greek mathematics. The existing codices are from Christian and Islamic times, which are sparingly supplemented by Egyptian papyrus notes. For the information about the formative years of Greek mathematics, we must rely entirely on small fragments transmitted by later authors and scattered remarks by philosophers and other not strictly mathematical authors. What we are able to present, is therefore, largely hypothetical, although somewhat consistent, picture of Greek mathematics, in its formative years.

The Greek victory over the Persian invasion resulted in the expansion and hegemony of Athens. Under Pericles, in the second half of the fifth century, democratic elements became influential. By 430 B.C., Athens became the leader of Greek empire, as well as the center of the Golden Age of Greece.

Another group of mathematically inclined philosophers were known as Pythagoreans, after their mythical founder of the school, Pythagoras. As to the Pythagoras' theorem, which the Pythagoreans ascribed its discovery to their master, we know that it was known in Hammurabi's Babylon. The most important discovery ascribed to the Pythagoreans was the discovery of the irrational by means of incommensurable line segments.

The period of Hellenism began with the conquests of Alexander the Great. When Alexander died at Babylon in 323 B.C., the whole Near East had fallen to the Greeks. Three empires emerged: Egypt under the Ptolemies; Mesopotamia and Syria under the Seleucids; and Macedonia under Antigonus. This close contact of Greek science with the Orient was extremely fertile. Practically all the really productive work which is called "Greek mathematics" was produced in the relatively short interval from 350-200 B.C. from Eudoxus to Apollonius; Even Eudoxus' achievements are known only through the interpretation by Euclid and Archimedes. It is interesting to note that the greatest flowering of the Hellenistic mathematics occurred in Egypt under the Ptolemies and not in Mesopotamia.

Among the first scholars associated with Alexandria, where Ptolemies built the famous library, was Euclid. Nothing is known with any certainty about Euclid's life. He probably flourished during the first Ptolemy (306-283 B.C.). Euclid's famous texts are the thirteen books of the Elements. No one knows how many of these texts are Euclid's own and how many are compilations. These thirteen books are the first mathematical texts preserved from Greek antiquity.

The greatest mathematician of the Hellenistic period was Archimedes (287-212 B.C.) who lived in Syracuse as advisor to King Hiero. His most important contribution was in the domain of what we now call "integral calculus" - theorems on areas of plane figures and on volumes of solid bodies. In measurement of the circle, Archimedes found an approximation of the circumference of the circle by the use of inscribed and circumscribed regular polygons. Typical of his rigor is the "Axiom of Archimedes." In his computational proficiency, Archimedes differed from most of the Greek mathematicians, which gave his work, a touch of the Oriental. This touch is revealed, for example, in his "Cattle Problem," a very complicated problem in indeterministic analysis, which may be interpreted as a problem leading to an equation of the "Pell" type $t^2 - 4729494u^2 = 1$, which is solved by very large numbers.

Alexandria remained the center of antique mathematics. Original work continued, although compilation and commentarization became more and more prominent form of science. It is wrong to believe that Alexandrian mathematics was purely "Greek" in the traditional Euclidean-Ptolemic sense; computational arithmetics and algebra of an Egyptian-Babylonian type were cultivated side by side with abstract geometrical demonstrations. We have to only think of Ptolemy, Heron and Diophantus to become convinced of this fact. Ptolemy, for example, found the value for π equal to 3.14166. In Metrica, Heron derived the formula for the area of a triangle

$$A = \sqrt{s(s-a)(s-b)(s-c)}$$

in purely geometric form, where $2s = a + b + c$. The Oriental touch is even stronger in the Arithmetica of Diophantus (250 A.D.) and we do not know who Diophantus was. He could be Babylonian.

The ancient civilization of the Near East never disappeared despite all Hellenistic influence. Both Oriental and Greek influences are clearly revealed in the science of Alexandria. Constantinople and India were also important meeting grounds of East and West.

The political hegemony of the Greeks over the Near East disappeared entirely with the sudden growth of Islam. After 622 A.D. the Arabs conquered large sections of Western Asia in an amazing sweep and before the end of the seventh century had occupied parts of the West Roman empire as far as Sicily, North Africa, and Spain. The Greco-Roman civilization was replaced by that of the Islam and the official language became Arabic instead of Greek or Latin.

With the decline of the Roman Empire, the center of mathematical research began to shift to India and later back to Mesopotamia. The first well preserved contributions to the exact sciences are the Siddhantas, of which Surya Siddhanta, is the original one (300-400 A.D.). These books deal mainly with astronomy and suggest the influence of Greek astronomy. They also indicate contact with Babylonian astronomy. Also, the Siddhantas show many native Indian characteristics. The Surya Siddhanta has tables of Sines (Jya) instead of chords. This sine is half-chord and hence is a line segment. From the fifth century A.D., names and books of individual Indian mathematicians have been preserved.

The best known mathematicians of India are Aryabhatta (500 A.D.) and Brahmagupta (625 A.D.). The question of their indebtedness to Greece, Babylon, and China is a subject of much conjecture. But they show at the same time much originality. Characteristics of their work are the arithmetical algebraic parts, which bear in their love for indeterminate equations some kinship to Diophantus. Aryabhatta had for π the value 3.1416. The first general solution of indeterministic equations of the first degree is found in Brahmagupta. It is therefore incorrect to call linear indeterminate equations Diophantine equations.

Around 1150 A.D., we find another excellent mathematician, Bhaskara. He solved, for example, $x^2 - 45x - 250 = 0$. His book, *Leelavati* was for many centuries a standard work on arithmetic and mensuration in the East. Ancient India may still yield many more mathematical treasures. We now know, for instance, that the Gregory-Leibnitz series for $\pi/4$ can already be found in a Sanskrit manuscript ascribed to Nilakanta (1500 A.D.).

The best known achievement of Hindu mathematics is our present decimal position system. The decimal system is very ancient, and so is the position system. But their combination appears in China and then in India. Its first Indian occurrence is on a plate of the year 595 A.D. where the date 346 is written in decimal place values system. There are early texts in which the word sunya, meaning zero, is explicitly used.

The mathematics of the Islamic period shows the same blend of influences familiar in Alexandria and in India. Islamic activities in the exact sciences, which began with Al-Fazari's translation of the Siddhantas, reached its first height with a native from Khiva,

Muhammad ibn Musa Al-Khwarizmi, who flourished about 825 A.D.
He wrote several books on mathematics and astronomy. His arithmetic
explained the Hindu system of numeration. A Latin translation of this
in the 12th century A.D. was the means by which Western Europe became acquainted with the decimal position. Muhammad's algebra had
the title Hisal al-jabar wal-muqabala (science of reduction and con-
frontation). This became known through Latin translations and they
made the word al-Jabr synonymous with the whole science of
"algebra." Also Muhammad's astronomical and trigonometrical tables
were translated into Latin. His geometry shows a definite lack of sym-
pathy with the Euclidean tradition. The works of Al-Khwarizmi as a
whole show Oriental rather than Greek influence. His work plays an
important role in the history of mathematics, because it is one of the
main sources through which Indian numerals and algebra came to
Western Europe. The Arabic astronomy was particularly interested in
trigonometry, the word "sinus" is a Latin translation of the Arabic
spelling of the Sanskrit "Jya."

The most advanced section of the Roman Empire from both an
economic and a cultural point of view had always been the East. The
West managed very well with a minimum of astronomy, arithmetic and
mensuration. But the stimulus to promote these sciences came from
the East. Leonardo, also called Fibonacci, was the first merchant
whose mathematical studies showed a certain maturity. He traveled in
the Orient as a merchant. On his return wrote his *Liber Abaci* (1202
A.D.) filled with arithmetical and algebraic information which he had
collected on his travels. Similarly, in his *Practica Geometriae* (1220
A.D.), Leonardo described whatever he had discovered in his travels in
geometry and trigonometry.

The rapid development of mathematics during the Renaissance
was due not only to the Rechenhaftigkeit of the commercial classes but
also to the productive use and further perfection of machines.
Machines were known to the Orient and to classical antiquity and they
had inspired the genius of Archimedes.

A general method of differentiation and integration, derived in the
full understanding that one process is the inverse of the other, could
only be discovered by men who mastered the geometrical method of
the Greeks as well as the algebraic method of Descartes. Such men

could have appeared only after 1660 A.D. and they actually did appear in Newton and Leibnitz. It is now established that both men found their methods independently of each other. Newton had calculus first (1605-66 A.D.) but Leibnitz published first (1673-76 A.D.). Leibnitz's school was far more brilliant than Newton's school. Our notation of the calculus is due to Leibnitz. Leibnitz's explanation of the foundations of calculus suffered from the same vagueness as Newton's. This vagueness was not removed until the modern limit concept was well established.

Chapter 2

Indifference to Truth

In this chapter, we shall summarize the contents of the research papers of A. Seidenberg, who traces the developments of the origin of mathematics. His work shows how the modern scholars have been continuously indifferent to the truth that the Greeks were not the inventors of geometric algebra. As a result, the prevailing view still remains, namely, that we owe geometry as a science to the genius of the Greeks.

Around 1900 A.D., the thesis that mathematics had a single origin would have been taken as a foregone conclusion, since there were no competitors to classical Greece. In fact, W.W.R. Ball wrote that "the history of mathematics cannot with certainty be traced back to any school or period before that of Ionian Greeks." This view was not entirely true, because there were the Sulvasutras, the sacred books on alter constructions of ancient India. Ball does not mention Sulvasutras but M. Cantor, a leading historian of mathematics of the day, had known of Sulvasutras. In 1875, G. Thibaut had translated a large portion of the Sulvasutras, which showed that Indian priests possessed significant mathematical knowledge. In 1877, Cantor, realizing the importance of Thibaut's work, began a comparative study of Greek and Indian mathematics.

Thibaut was a Sanskrit scholar and his principal objective was to make available to the learned world, the mathematical knowledge of the Vedic Indians. After commenting that a good deal of Indian knowledge could be traced back to requirements of ritual, Thibaut adds that these facts have a double interest.

> In the first place, they are valuable for the history of the human mind in general. In the second place, they are important for the mental history of India and for answering the question relative to the originality of Indian science. For whatever is closely connected with the ancient Indian religion must be considered as having sprung up among the Indians themselves, unless positive evidence of the strongest kind point to the contrary conclusion.

Thibaut did not formulate the obvious conclusion, namely, that the Greeks were not the inventors of plane geometry, rather it was Indians. Nonetheless, this was the message that the Greek scholars saw in Thibaut's paper. They clearly did not like it. If Indians invented plane geometry, what was to become of Greek "genius" or Greek "miracle" was the question. Most of the refutations were mere haughty dismissals. But Cantor concluded that Indian geometry and Greek geometry, especially of Heron, are related. Since Thibaut in 1875 did not assign an absolute date to the Sulvasutras, Cantor was free to press his own chronology. He assigned 100 B.C. to Sulvasutras and expressed an opinion that the Indians were, in geometry, the pupils of the Greeks. Cantor eventually renounced his view and conceded a much earlier date to Indian geometry. Even so, he did not believe that Pythagoras got his geometry from India. He preferred to believe it was Egypt. A. Weber and A.B. Keith also disputed a connection between Sulvasutras and the older sacred literature and denied that it showed any knowledge of geometry.

In 1899, Thibaut ventured to assign the fourth or the third centuries B.C. as the possible date for the composition of Sulvasutras. But he made a concession to Cantor, by saying that "there is nothing striking in the independent development of a limited amount of practical knowledge by two different peoples." A "limited amount of practical knowledge," what a terrible statement!

In 1910, A. Burk translated the Sulvasutras of Apastamba, with a commentary, which does not make any original points. Anyway, the damage had been done and the Sulvasutras have never taken the position in the history of mathematics that they deserve. E.T. Bell in his *Development of Mathematics* and B.L. van der Warden in his *Science Awakening* do not so much as even mention Sulvasutras. Thus Vedic geometrical knowledge faded into insignificance.

The Greeks themselves had supposed or conjectured, that they had received their intellectual capital, especially in geometry, from the more Ancient East, but modern historians have been hard put to corroborate their views. Consequently, the prevailing view was and still remains that we owe geometry as a science to the genius of the Greeks.

In 1928, O. Neugebauer disclosed the existence of the theorem of Pythagoras well over a thousand years before Pythagoras in old Babylonian mathematical texts. He also suggested a direct borrowing by the Greeks and Indians from a common origin in Babylonia. The problem with this suggestion is that many of the common elements of Greek and Indian mathematics, especially in the geometrical constructions which are at issue, are not found in old Babylonia. The monumental translation work of Neugebauer of old Babylonian mathematical texts quite transformed our notions of ancient mathematics, at least for Babylonia. "What is called Pythagorean in the Greek tradition had better be called Babylonian", wrote Neugebauer in 1937. Because of this, the old notion that mathematics started in Greece in the sixth century B.C. is gone. However, Neugebauer's view of the origin of geometry was the prevailing view already described. What he noted was the dominant aspect of old Babylonian mathematics, namely, its computational character.

Basing himself on the work of Neugebauer and Zeuthen, Van der Warden expounded the view that Babylonian mathematics was the basis of Greek mathematics with great clarity and cogency. Not everyone found attractive the theory of Neugebauer and van der Warden. M.S. Mahoney in 1934 wrote that "he would rather invoke the Greek miracle than assume that Babylonian mathematics was a basis for Greek developments and the vast promise of pre-Greek mathematics is, to a large extent, illusory." Neugebauer's views did meet with criticism and queries, even when the main issue, whether Greece borrowed from Babylonians, is clear enough.

It can be seen that the Babylonian treatment of quadratic equations and that of the Greeks are related. Hence Van der Warden, concluded that the Babylonian procedures were certainly the basis for the Greek developments. He should have concluded that they have a common source, but not that the source is certainly Babylonia.

S. Unguru in 1975 has used an amazing trick to show that "its all an illusion! The modern mathematicians, turned historians, look at ancient mathematics through modern literal eyeglasses, and see things that are not there." If Unguru is right, what Van der Warden and Neugebauer and their predecessors, said is utter nonsense. Van der Warden provided an ingenious refutation of Unguru's trick. However, if one includes the Vedic mathematics, in addition to Babylonia, one will get a different perspective on ancient mathematics.

The main issue is the origin of geometric algebra. The Sulvasutras have geometric algebra and one can show that Greece and India have a common heritage that cannot be derived from old Babylonia, namely, the old Babylonia of about 1700 B.C., as portrayed in Science Awakening of Van der Warden.

The Indian priests in their altar rituals had to convert a rectangle into a square.

> If you wish to turn an oblong into a square, take the tiyanmani (the shorter side of the oblong) for the side of the square, divide the remainder (that part of the oblong which remains after the square has been cut off) into two parts and inverting (one of them) join these two parts to the sides of the square. (We get then a large square out of which a small square is cut out as it were.) Fill the empty space (in the corner) by adding a small piece (a small square). It has been taught how to deduct it (the added piece).

(See Baudhayana Sulvasutras I 54, Apastamba Sulvasutra II 7 or Katyayana Sulvasutra III 2.) This is entirely in the spirit of the Elements, Book II. The theorem of Pythagoras and the identity

$$xy = \left(\tfrac{x+y}{2}\right)^2 - \left(\tfrac{x-y}{2}\right)^2$$

are the key facts in the solutions. The old Babylonians could have no use for such a procedure. They would simply multiply the two sides and take the square root.

The Sulvasutras contain all the geometrical details. Nowhere they say they are being original. They insist that they are doing things as it has been taught, in the Samhitas and Brahmanas and both come before Sulvasutras. The Rig-Veda is still earlier. In the Sulvasutra, the construction of alters of various shapes is described, the shape depending on the particular ritual. Thus there are square alters, circular alters, and alters of many other shapes, such as example, the falcon shaped alter and the Mahavedi. Mahavedi is an isosceles trapezoid having bases 24 and 30 and width 36. The Saptapatha Brahmana and the Taittiriya Samhita both explicitly give the dimensions of Mahavedi. Not only Vedic priests compute the area of Mahavedi but also show how to get the answer. See Figure 2.1.

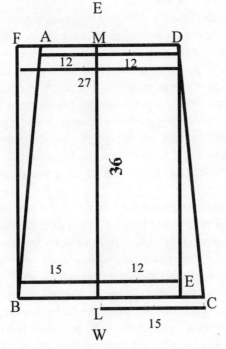

Figure 2.1: Area of Mahavedi

To establish this, Apastamba Sulvasutra V 7 says,

> one draws (a line) from the southern amsa (D in Figure 2.1) toward
> to the southern sroni (C), namely to (the point E) which is 12 padas
> from the point L of the prsthya. Thereupon one turns the piece cut
> off (that is, the triangle DEC) around and carries it to the other side
> (that is, to the north). Thus the Vedi obtains the form of a
> rectangle. In this form (FBED) one computes its area which is 972
> square units.

The striking thing here is that we have the proof. Many scholars
who refer to the Sulvasutras claim that there are no proofs there. We
can only suppose that these scholars have not bothered to examine the
work but are guided by a common belief that Oriental mathematics
does not present arguments for proof but only prescribe certain rules.
If one looks, one finds several proofs.

Let us consider next the theory of Pythagoras under two aspects.
In Aspect I, the theorem is employed to construct the side of a square
equal to the sum or difference of two squares. In Aspect II, the theorem is used to compute the diagonal of a rectangle. Aspect II comes in,
for example, when one uses the (3, 4, 5) triangle to construct a right
angle. The Sulvasutras know both aspects. The Elements has only Aspect I, but classical Greek geometry presumably also realized Aspect
II, since it had Pythagorean number triples. The old Babylonians had
Aspect II, but they would have had no use for Aspect I. They would
simply square the lengths of the sides of the given squares, add and
take the square root.

One could give further common elements of the Greek and Indian
mathematics not shared by old Babylonia. For example, the gnomon or
the problem of squaring the circle. In Apastamba Sulvasutra III 9 and
in the Elements II 4, the gnomon is analyzed into two rectangles and a
square, and the propositions amount to our rule $(a + b)^2 = a^2 + b^2 + 2ab$. The squaring of the circle is a true geometrical problem in Greece
and in India. The conclusion one can make therefore is either the geo-
metric algebra of Greece came from India or that of India came from
Greece or both came from a third source different from old Babylonia
of 1700 B.C.

There are several grounds on which the second of these alternatives, namely, the geometric algebra of India came from Greece, has to be eliminated. First there is the chronology. Clearly, Saptapatha Brahmana and hence geometric algebra goes back to before the 6th century B.C. Moreover, *Inde Classique* by L. Renou and J. Filliozat, places the Saptapatha Brahmana at 1000-800 B.C. If one accepts the chronology mentioned above, then we cannot maintain Van der Warden and Neugebauer's thesis on the generation of geometric algebra, for geometric algebra existed in India before the classical period in Greece.

There is another argument independent of Indian chronology. It is the idea that geometric algebra was developed as a way to meet the crisis of the discovery of non-commensurables. For, if this is the way things went, then the Indian priests seized on a technical point in mathematics and made it the central feature of their theologic geometry. This is too hard to believe.

Let us sum up the arguments. A comparison of Pythagorean and Vedic mathematics together with some chronological considerations show that the current view on the generation of geometric algebra is not tenable. A common source for the Pythagorean and Vedic mathematics is to be sought either in the Vedic mathematics or in an older mathematics very much like it. The view that Vedic mathematics is a derivative of old Babylonian has been rejected. What are regarded as the two main sources of Western mathematics, namely, Pythagorean and old Babylonian mathematics, both flow from a still older source. This old common source must be very much like what we see in the Sulvasutras. In the first place, it was associated with ritual. Second, there was no dichotomy between number and magnitude. It did not assign a number to the diagonal of a unit square, because it did not know what the number was. In geometry, it knew the theorem of Pythagoras and how to convert a rectangle into a square. It knew the isosceles trapezoid and how to compute its area. It had facility with whole numbers and knew some number theory centered on the existence of Pythagorean principles. It had the canonical solution for the circulature of the square, and in its attempts to square the circle, it learned how to compute a square root.

Chapter 3

Invented Theories

When we examine the standard books on World history today, we discover that they are largely devoted to the history of modern Europe, with the history of non-European cultures turned into a
mere footnote. Moreover, the Western scholarship on India was influenced not only by the prevalent European historical and philosophical methodologies but also by colonial interest. Such attitudes still prevail.

In the late 18th century many Sanskrit classics, including the Bhagavad Gita, were first translated into contemporary European languages. William Jones began his study of Sanskrit and
soon noticed remarkable similarities between Sanskrit and European languages such as Greek and Latin. It was Jones who first laid the foundation in 1774 A.D. for the Western history of ancient India. Refusing to recognize that the culture and civilization of Bharat (ancient India is called Bharat) existed for about 6000 years before 327 B.C., Jones concluded that "the first ages of the Hindus are chiefly mythological and thus the historical age of India cannot be carried further back to two thousand years before Christ." As a result, he deliberately created the problem of two Chandraguptas and reduced by more than 1200

years the chronology of the Magadha dynasties of India. Jones mis-
identified Chandragupta Maurya (1534-1500 B.C.) of Maurya Dynasty
with Chandragupta (327-320 B.C.) of the Imperial Gupta dynasty.
Since then Jones and Orientalists propagated continuously this erroneous identification in Asiatic researches and other journals to give a
definite stamp to his theory.

To account for the common origin of Sanskrit and the European
languages, European scholars also invented a hypothesis that an Aryan
invasion of India occurred in ancient times by people who spoke early
Indo-European language. In picking the date of the assumed invasion
of India, called the "Aryan invasion of India," Max Müller was strong-
ly influenced by the Christian belief that the creation of the world took
place in 4004 B.C. Supposing this date, Müller chose 2448 B.C. for
the biblical flood, leaving 1000 years for the water to subside and the
land to dry enough for the Aryans to begin their invasion of India
around 1400 B.C. He then added 200 years to allow for the composition of the Rig Veda around 1200 B.C. This is what is known as historical research by the so-called objective scholars of the West, whom
the Indian historians have been blindly following.

The theory of Aryan invasion is that the Aryans originated not
from Bharat but from elsewhere. However, the historians do not point
to any single region as the homeland of the Aryans. At the last count,
they did indicate more than twenty zones in the West and in the North
from which the Aryans could have sprung. Even the North Pole was
proposed as the Aryan abode.

Unfortunately, not a single region proposed by the scholars
showed even the slightest link with the high civilization and classical
art and literature of Bharat. The doubts of the historians should have
vanished with the findings of excavations of Mohenjodaro and
Harappa, known as the Indus Valley civilization in the early 20th century. The excavations clearly show a flourishing civilization that existed thousands of years ago, distinct from all others, independent and
deeply rooted in the Indian soil and environment. Faced with this evidence, the historians had to admit that the pre-Aryan Indus Valley civilization, with no known beginnings, was highly developed, thoroughly
individual, and essentially Aryan. Moreover, recent excavations show
that it is so vast that it encompassed a staggering one and a half million

square kilometers, an area larger than Western Europe. This civilization had its own distinctive style proving an expression of Indian genius. It is as if the present were the past and not much had changed despite the passage time. Nonetheless, these historians maintain that the Aryans did not spring from the indigenous culture of India but were from a different culture and arrived, somehow, from somewhere else, at a later stage.

All the misconceptions in the history of the human past and the arbitrary fixed Indian history have their root in one fixed idea that everything really great in India has been introduced by foreigners. This persistent habit of looking outside of India for the origin of everything has resulted in many false conclusions.

Many Indian historians have passively accepted the misrepresentation of their culture and history because the eminent historians of Europe have concluded so. Since Indian historians agree with the assessment of the Western historians, they are happy in turn with the spirit of international cooperation. Consequently, the textbooks on Indian history still taught in schools and colleges reflect these cooked-up views as proven history.

The speculative assumption that Maurya Chandragupta (1534-1500 B.C.) was the contemporary of Alexander, which was proposed by Jones and later supported by Müller, has created many absurdities, because other incorrect conclusions have been drawn from it. These conclusions have resulted in turn in many misconceptions about ancient Indian chronology and also about our ancient past. The famous Buddha, for example, lived during 1887 to 1807 B.C. and not in 563-483 B.C. as was adopted. The Buddhistic works report that Buddha was 72 years old at the coronation of Ajatasatru in 1814 B.C., who belongs to Sisunaga dynasty of Magadha empire. Also, Buddha was contemporary of Kshemajit and Bimbisara of the same dynasty. In The *Heritage of India* series, Kenneth J. Sanders (1922 edition) writes "when Ajatasatru came to the throne of Magadha, Gautama Buddha was 72 years old, but his genius still shone bright and clear." Buddha attained Nirvana when he was 80 years old. Thus he lived during 1887-1807 B.C. E.J. Rapson in Ancient India Vol. I, warns that "we are still uncertain as to the exact date of the birth of Buddha. The date 483 B.C., which was adopted in history as the date of Nirvana of

Buddha, must still be regarded as provisional." Despite the warning, the provisionally fixed date of Buddha (563-483 B.C.) is taken as proven fact. In fact, it was Sankara who lived during 509-477 B.C. and who was responsible for overthrowing the decadent Buddhistic faith from India and re-establishing Sanatana Dharma, the so-called Hinduism.

Maurya Chandragupta's (1534-1500 B.C.) grandson was the famous Asoka (or Asokavardhana) of Maurya dynasty. Asoka ruled the Magadha empire during 1472-1436 B.C. for 36 years. At that time there were no Greek states in the region of modern Greece.

At the time of Asoka Maurya (1472-1436 B.C.) there were five kingdoms of "Yavanas" in Northwest India; namely, Abhisara, Uraga, Simhapura, Divyakataka and Uttarajyotish, which were subordinate to him. "Yavana" is a Sanskrit word. "Yona" or "Yauna" are the Prakrit forms derived from it. We find the expression "Yona Laja" is the inscriptions of Asoka Maurya. "Ra" in Sanskrit is pronounced as "La" in Prakrit, just as "Sa" is pronounced as "Ha." Thus "Raja" in Sanskrit becomes "Laja" in Prakrit. Similarly Sarasvati becomes Halahati, Yavana becomes Yona and so on.

In Mahabharata war (3138 B.C.), the Sakas, Yavanas and other Dasyu kings of Northwest of Bharata Varsha (greater India) fought on Kaurava's side who lost the war. The survivors of these kingdoms of Northwest Bharat, then migrated to Western Asia and further west to Europe. The Yavanas were prominent among these migrants. The region where they settled down in Asia Minor and Europe was called after them "Ionia" and the settlers came to be known as "Ionians." Later around 1000 B.C., nomadic tribes inhabiting the forest region of Northwestern Europe, descended and occupied the country as a ruling race. The Greeks are therefore the descendants of mixed descent, of the conquering Greek invaders and the native civilized Ionians. They called themselves Greeks and their land Greece. In the fifth century B.C., all the Ionian denominations were abolished by a legislative decree and the term "Greek" was alone compulsorily employed for all the population. In the subsequent writings, therefore, we find only the term Greek and never the Ionians. The 19th century European historians of India, began to interpret the terms Yavana and Yona in the literature of India to mean Greek and Indo-Greek. Clearly, there were no Greeks in

Asoka Maurya's time and Yavanas or Yonas were not Greeks. In fact, there was Yavana kingdom in South India with the capital city called Yavana Pura and also in East India near Assam. The authentic Greek history begins with Phillip, the father of Alexander. The so-called history of the previous times is full of ambiguities, conjectures and fanciful tales.

Recently there have appeared several scholarly works dismissing the theory of Aryan invasion and correcting the chronology of ancient Bharat, even though this has not yet entered into the standard books and school texts. For example, see the works of Apte, Feuerstein, Frawley, Kak, Lakshmikantham, Rajaram, Rangachary, Sethna, Talageri and Venkatachalam. As a result, those who receive the western education, only see the European view of the world history and implicitly believe that everything they read in the standard books is absolutely true.

Vedic literature consists of fourteen main sacred scriptures, namely, the four Vedas, the six Vedangas and four Upangas. The four Vedas, Rig, Yajur, Sama and Atharva that are existing now were codified more than 5000 years ago, before the beginning of Kali Yuga (astronomical cycle which started in 3102 B.C.) by Veda Vyasa and his disciples Paila, Vaisampayana, Jaimini and Sumanthu. Vyasa's given name was Krishna Dvaipayana. His compilation consisted of 1131 Sakhas (recessions) and at present time only 10 Sakhas are available. Samhita portion of the Vedas is the main text of Vedas. The second portion of Sakha is Brahmana and the third portion of sakha is Aranyaka. The Upanishads come after Aranyakas. Sulvasutras form the part of Vedanagas which belong to the part of the Kalpa Vedanga. Among the nine Sulvasutra texts, the three Sulvasutras of Baudhayana, Apastamba and Katyayana are most important from the point of view of mathematical contribution. The word Sulva is derived from the verb, "Sulv" which means "to measure." Some statements in Sulvasutras are taken directly from Taithiriya Samhita, Saptapatha Brahmana and Aranyakas.

In Vedic scriptures are given several cosmic cycles to measure time. The day, the week, the month and the year (lunar as well as solar) are very well known to us. The other important cosmic cycles are:

1. 60-year Jovian cycle,
2. 2700 year cycle of Sapta Rishis (related to the Big Bear),
3. 27000 year cycle of the asterisms called the Great Year or the precession cycle,
4. 432,000 year cycle called a yuga
5. $4 \cdot 32 \times 10^6$-year cycle known as Mahayuga, and
6. Kalpa, the cycle consisting of $4 \cdot 32 \times 10^9$ years.

All these cosmic cycles are related to our solar system and have the astronomical basis which can be verified. The present yuga called the Kali Yuga has stared in 3102 B.C. and its duration is 432,000 years as noted above. According to the computation given in Surya Siddhanta, Vishnu Purana, Mahabharata and Manu Smirithi, the time duration from the present creation of our solar system up to 2000 A.D., is 1,972,949,102 years. (Deducting 17,064,000 years that were taken in creating animate and inanimate beings before the existing order of things, we get, 1,955,885,102 years since the beginning of the humanity.) We also learn that 123,261,102 years ago, violent changes of cataclysmic nature occurred with high water level covering the entire Earth. Surya Siddhanta states that it was written when the recent Krita Yuga was still 1200 years to go, which computes up to 2000 A.D., a life of 2,166,302 years for Surya Siddhanta. Many commentaries of Surya Siddhanta were reported by Varahamihira, the great astronomer, in his Pancha Siddhanta and he lived in the first century B.C.

The Imperial Gupta dynasty, which started with Chandragupta I in 327 B.C. ended in 82 B.C. with the last emperor Kumaragupta. After the dynasty of Imperial Guptas, the Panwar dynasty came into prominence from 82 B.C. (3020 Kali Era) with the famous emperor Vikramaditya. He conquered all of India as far as Herat and founded Vikrama Era in 57 B.C. (3045 Kali Era). In Vikramaditya's court, there were Nava Ratnas (nine gems) of whom Varahamihira, the great astronomer was one. He wrote Pancha Siddhanta in 123 B.C. in which he codified the five existing Siddhantas (astronomical works) related to the present Mahayuga. After the demise of Vikramaditya in 18 A.D. (3120 Kali Era), the empire was split into eighteen states and there were invasions from Sakas, Tartars and other Dasyu kings. After sixty years, the great grandson of Vikramaditya, namely, Salivahana conquered and recovered the plundered booty from the invaders. This great and mighty emperor established Salivahana Era in 78 A.D. (3180 Kali Era). Before these two eras, the Cyrus Era was prevalent in Northwest India whose empire stretched up to Punjab in India. Cyrus was the Saka king of Persia who founded the Cyrus Era in 550 B.C. (2552 Kali Era). Astronomer Varhamihira, in his Brihat Samhita made use of the Era of Cyrus and explained how to compute it. This era was known as Saka Kala and Sakanripa Kala, meaning the time of Saka king.

The modern period starts in India from the time of Mahabharata war in 3138 B.C., thirty six years before Kali Yuga that commenced in 3102 B.C. We find detailed information of dynasties including the names of the kings in each dynasty and the corresponding duration of their reign. At the end of Mahabharata war, the victorious Yudhistira of the Pandavas was crowned the emperor of Bharata Varsha (Greater India) at Hastinapura. Thus, Yudhistira Era began in 3138 B.C. The Sapta Rishi Era began in 3076 B.C. (26 Kali Era), which was the year of demise of Yudhistira, when Sapta Rishi Mandala (the Big Bear) left the star Magha. This era is also known as Loukikabda Era as well as Svargarohana (ascent to heaven) time of Yudhistira.

When Ptolemy, the great second century astronomer, mathematician and geographer of Alexandria, produced the first scientific geography and drafted the global map, he must have had in front of him a manuscript of the Periplus. In this map, India was shown as a country extending East and West, Asia and Africa were joined together to make one continent and Indian Ocean was merely an island sea. Although western historians discounted it as a distortion, this map confirms the Vedic description of Bharata Varsha (the greater India) and the formation of Indian Ocean later.

Bharata Varsha has existed for thousands of years peacefully. Activity in all spheres of life prevailed in Bharat, when even Greece did not exist, when Rome was not thought of, when the very fathers of modern Europeans lived in the forests and painted themselves blue. Even earlier, when history has no record and tradition dares not peer into the gloom of that distant past, idea after idea marched out from Bharat, every word spoken with a blessing behind it and peace after it. India has never been a conquering nation. With that blessing on its head, India lives.

Chapter 4

Chronological Aspects

In the modern period of Bharat (India), Aryabhatta is the first famous mathematician and astronomer. In his book *Aryabhatteeyam*, Aryabhatta clearly provides his birth data. In 10th stanza, he says that when $60 \times 6 = 360$ years elapsed in this Kali Yuga, he was 23 years old. The stanza of the sloka starts with "Shastyabdanam Shadbhiryada vyateetastra yascha yuga padah." "Shastyabdanam Shadbhi" means $60 \times 6 = 360$. While printing the manuscript, the word "Shadbhi" was altered to "Shasti", which implies $60 \times 60 = 3600$ years after Kali Era. As a result of this intentional arbitrary change, Aryabhatta's birth time was fixed as 476 A.D. Since in every genuine manuscript, we find the word "Shadbhi" and not the altered "Shasti", it is clear that Aryabhatta was 23 years old in 360 Kali Era or 2742 B.C. This implies that Aryabhatta was born in 337 Kali Era or 2765 B.C. and therefore could not have lived around 500 A.D., as manufactured by the Indologists to fit their invented framework.

Bhaskara I is the earliest known commentator of Aryabhatta's works. His exact time is not known except that he was in between Aryabhatta (2675 B.C.) and Varahamihira (123 B.C.).

Bhaskara mentions the names of Latadeva, Nisanku and Panduranga Svami as disciples of Aryabhatta. Moreover, he says that Aryabhatta's

27

fame has crossed the bounds of the oceans and whose works lead to accurate results even after lapse of so much time. This shows that Bhaskara I was living quite a lot of time later than Aryabhatta. His works are Maha Bhaskariyam, Aryabhatteeya Bhashyam and Laghu Bhaskariyam.

Next is Varahamihira who says that he was writing his Pancha Siddhanta in the year 427 Saka Kala. Since Saka Kala or Saka Era, started in 550 B.C., it means that $550 - 427 = 123$ B.C. Varahamihira also indicates how to find Saka Kala in Brihat Samhita, which is equal to the Svargarohana time of Yudhistira coupled with 2526 years, that is $3076 - 2526 = 550$ B.C. Svargarohana time of Yudhistira is 26 years after Kali Era and therefore $26 + 2526 = 2552$ Kali Era is the starting point of Saka Kala or Sakanripa Kala. Thus the Cyrus Era which was in vogue in Varahamihira's time began in 550 B.C. and Cyrus the Great was the Persian Saka King. The special contribution of Varahamihira was Pancha Siddhanta in which he codified the then existing five Siddhantas, namely, Paulisa, Romaka, Vasista, Surya (Saura) and Pitamaha. In addition, he wrote the famous Brihat Samhita, the theoretical and predictive astrology. Only Surya Siddhanta has been preserved. Varahamihira quotes a tribute paid to a Yavana (not Greek) astronomer, by an early astronomer Garga, namely, "the Yavanas are Mlechchas (people deviated from Sanatana Dharma) but amongst them this science of astronomy is duly established and therefore they are honored as Rishis." Recall that there were Yavana kingdoms in South and North-west of India even before Maurya Asoka's time (1472-1436 B.C.). At that time, there were no Greeks. This tribute to Yavanas has been mis-interpreted in the literature to imply the influence of Greek astronomy on Indian astronomy in Garga's time. Since Garga's time was long be-fore Varahamihira's time and since Yavanas were not Greeks at that time, the conclusion of the influence of Greek astronomy on the astro-nomy of ancient India has no validity.

After Bhaskara I, we have Brahmagupta, who is a great mathe-matician and astronomer. According to Brahmagupta, he completed his work Brahma Siddhanta when he was 30 years of age in 550 Saka Kala. This means Brahmagupta was born in 30 B.C.

Next in line of astronomers and mathematical thinkers was Bhaskaracharya, known as Bhaskara II, who is the author of a popular work called Siddhanta Siromani. He states that he compiled his work in 1036 Sakanripakala (the time of Saka king). Hence subtracting 550 from 1036, we get 486 A.D. as the time of compilation of Siddhanta Siromani.

We have seen that Saka Kala or Sakanripa Kala is the Cyrus Era which started in 550 B.C. (2552 Kali Era) and was in vogue in Northern India. Our modern historians have taken Saka Kala to mean Salivahana Saka which started in 78 A.D. The same scholars have rejected the existence of Vikramaditya and his great grandson, Salivahana who are traditionally well known great and powerful emperors. Nonetheless, they resurrected Salivahana from his nonexistence only to utilize his era 78 A.D. so as to establish their preconceived notion that mathematical texts do not exist in India before the Christian Era and to fit the evidence in their fabricated chronology. In the *Oxford Student's History of India*, 1915 edition, V.A. Smith proclaims, for example, that "opinions differ, but it is probable that the Saka Era 78 A.D. dates from the coronation of Kanishka, the Saka king. In later years, the era was known as that of Salivahana." But Kanishka was not a Saka king but was a Turushka who ruled Kashmir. His coronation was in 1224 B.C. It was Cyrus who was a Saka king and whose empire stretched up to Punjab in India. Moreover, the statement that Kanishka's era in later years was known as Salivahana era is a very bold guess indeed with no substance. Thus the times of Varahamihira, Brahmagupta and Bhaskara II were all fixed relative to Salivahana Era 78 A.D. even though they all clearly say that it was Saka Kala (the Cyrus Era) they are referring to. Note also, Varahamihira has described the method of computing Saka Kala from Kali Era 3102 B.C. As a result, the standard books and others who follow them accept the cooked-up times of mathematicians, astronomers and prominent figures as proven facts. We shall give below the list of actual times of important persons for a quick reference.

Birth of	Veda Vyasa	3374 B.C.
	Baudhayana	3200 B.C.
Birth of	Aryabhatta	2765 B.C.
	Buddha's time	1888-1807 B.C.
Coronation of	Chandragupta Maurya	1554 B.C.
Coronation of	Asoka Maurya	1472 B.C.
	Kanishka's time	1294-1234 B.C.
Coronation of	Chandragupta of	
	Imperial Gupta Dynasty	327 B.C.
	Varahamihira wrote	
	Pancha Siddhanta	123 B.C.
	Vikramaditya's time	102 B.C. to 78 A.D.
Birth of	Bhahmagupta	30 B.C.
	Salivahana Era	78 A.D.
	Bhaskara II wrote	
	Siddhanta Siromani	486 A.D.

Chapter 5

From Baudhayana to Bhaskara I

Recall that Sulvasutras belong to that part of Vedic scriptures known as Vedangas and Sulvasutras of Baudhayana, Apastamba and Katyayana are important ancient texts which use mathematical results. Pundit Venkatachalam (1885-1959 A.D.) proved that Baudhayana lived during 3200 B.C. Also, Samhitas, Brahmanas and Aranyakas of Vedic literature were earlier than Sulvasutras.

In the Yajur Veda Samhita the powers of 10 such as sata (100), sahastra (1000) and so on up to 10 raised to the power 12, known as parardha, have been mentioned. The same list appears in Taittiriya Samhita. Moreover, following the decimal base system, compound numbers for example, 19 and 972 have been conveniently referred as ekona vimsati (one less than 20) and astavimsatyunam sahasram (28 less than 1000). Even Rig Veda indicates fractions such as one-half, one-eighth and one sixteenth and so on.

The following geometrical results are either explicitly mentioned or clearly implied in the construction of the alters of the prescribed shapes and sizes in Sulvasutras.

(a) The diagonals of a rectangle bisect each other. They divide the rectangle into four parts which are identical.

(b)   The isosceles triangle is divided into two identical halves by the line joining the vertex to the middle point of the base.

(c)   The quadrilateral formed by the lines joining the middle points of the sides of a rectangle is a rhombus whose area is half of that of the rectangle.

(d)   A parallelogram and rectangle on the same base and within the same parallels have the same area.

(e)   The square on the hypotenuse of a right angle triangle is equal to the sum of the squares on the other two sides.

(f)   If the sum of the squares on two sides of a triangle is equal to the square on the third side, then the triangle is right angled.

(g)   The diagonal of a rectangle produces both areas which its length and breadth produce separately.

We note that (e) and (f) are the so-called Pythagoras Theorem and its converse respectively.

Also, the following geometrical constructions are used in Sulvasutras:

(i)   To divide a circle into any number of equal areas by drawing diameters.

(ii)   To divide a triangle into a number of equal and similar areas.

(iii) To draw a straight line at right angles to a given line from a given point.

(iv)   To construct an isosceles trapezium of given altitude, face and base.

(v)   To construct a square equal to the sum of two different squares.

(vi)   To construct a triangle equivalent to a given square.

(vii) To construct a rhombus equivalent to a given square or a rectangle.

(viii) To construct an isosceles trapezium having a given face and equivalent to a given square or a rectangle.

In the Sulvasutras, we find not only the squaring of the circle, but also the reverse problem of turning of the square into a circle. This is done as follows (see Figure 5.1).

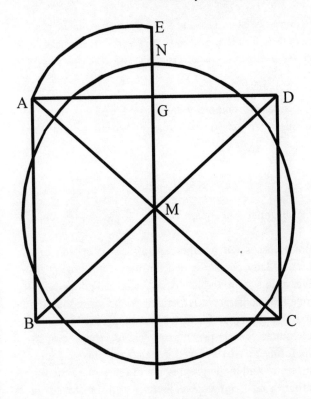

Figure 5.1: Squaring the Circle

In square ABCD, let M be the intersection of the diagonals. Draw the circle with M as center and MA as radius, and let ME be a radius of this circle perpendicular to AD and cutting AD at G. Let $GN = \frac{1}{3}GE$. Then MN is the radius of a circle having area equal to the square ABCD. (Taking MG = 1). This comes to saying that

$$\pi(1 + \tfrac{\sqrt{2}-1}{3})^2 = 4 \text{ or } \pi = (\tfrac{6}{2+\sqrt{2}})^2.$$

For the reverse problem, that of squaring the circle, we are given the rule:

If you wish to turn a circle into a square, divide the diameter into 8 parts, and again one of these 8 parts into 29 parts; of these 29 parts remove 28, and moreover, the sixth part (of the one part left) less the eighth part (of the sixth part).

The meaning is: side of required square $= \frac{7}{8} + \frac{1}{8 \times 29} - \frac{1}{8 \times 29 \times 6} + \frac{1}{8 \times 29 \times 6 \times 8}$ of the diameter of given circle. We also find the approximation

$$\sqrt{2} = 1 + \frac{1}{3} + \frac{1}{3 \times 4} - \frac{1}{3 \times 4 \times 34}.$$

More precisely, the diagonal of a square $= 1 + \frac{1}{3} + \frac{1}{3 \times 4} - \frac{1}{3 \times 4 \times 34}$ of a side.

There was some discussion whether Sulvasutras knew the irrationality of the $\sqrt{2}$. Many people denied but they were always inclined to deny everything from India. Apastamba categorically observes that the circle thus constructed is "anitya" in the sense that it is "inexact" or approximate. It is therefore good enough proof.

Again, in Sulvasutras, we can find the problem of solving quadratic equations of the form $ax^2 + bx + c = 0$ is stated and solved. Moreover, several examples of arithmetic progression (Samanantara Sredhi) and geometric progression (Gunottama Sredhi) can be found in Taittiriya Samhita, Saptapatha Brahmana and Baudhayana Sulvasutra. We also find the solutions of the first degree indeterminate equations.

The father of scientific astronomy was Aryabhatta (born in 2765 B.C.); who was teaching astronomy and mathematics when he was 23 years of age in 2742 B.C. His astronomical knowledge was so advanced that he could claim that the Earth rotated on its own axis and was able to calculate the epicycles and eccentric circles and the position and course of the planets. He declared "the spotless jewel of true knowledge which lay so long sunk in the ocean of knowledge, both true and false, has been raised by me, therefrom, using the boat of my intelligence." In his Aryabhattiyam, Aryabhatta included a special section "ganita" on pure mathematics. He described various original ways to perform different mathematical operations, including square and cube roots and solving quadratic equations. He made use of decimals, the zero and the place value system.

To find an approximate value of the ratio of the circumference of a circle to its diameter (usually denoted by π), Aryabhatta gives the following prescription.

Add 4 to 100, multiply by 8 and add to 62,000. This is approximately the circumference of a circle whose diameter is 20,000. This means $\pi = \frac{62,832}{20,000} = 3.1416$. It is important to note that Aryabhatta indicates that this value is approximate which is a rational explanation to suggest that π is incommensurable or irrational.

Before we proceed with the information of the sine tables according to Aryabhatta, let us see how the trigonometric ratios are defined in ancient Indian mathematics. The name for trigonometry in Indian astronomy is Jyotpathi ganita, which literally means (Jya+Utpathi) mathematics of construction or generating sines. The ancient Indian astronomers used generally three functions namely, Jya, Kotijya and Utkramajya (sine, cosine and versed sine). Recall that the word "sinus" is a Latin translation of the Arabic spelling of Sanskrit word "Jya." It is important to remember that the trigonometric ratios in Indian astronomy are with reference to an arc of a circle rather than an angle.

In Figure 5.2, consider an arc ANB of a circle of radius R centered at O. Since the arc ANB looks like a bow, it is called dhanus (bow) and the chord AMB is called Jya (bowstring). The half-chord is referred to as ardha-Jya (half-chord). In due course, the half-chord came to be known as Jya itself. Define Jya of arc AN = AM, Kotijya of arc AN = OM and Utkrama Jya of arc AN = MN.

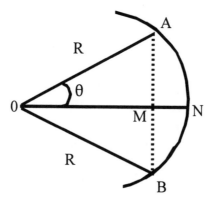

Figure 5.2: The Jya

If θ is the angle subtended by arc AN at the center of the circle, then from the current trigonometry, we get AM = R sin θ and OM = R cos θ, and therefore, Jya(θ) = R sin θ, Kotijya(θ) = R cos θ and Utkrama Jya(θ) = ON − OM = R − R cos θ = R(1 − cos θ) = R versin θ.

The radius R is taken as approximately 3438; this is because, taking the angular measure of the circle as 360 degrees or 360 × 60 = 21,600 minutes, one gets

$$R = \frac{21600}{2\pi} = \frac{21600}{2(3.1416)} = 3438 \text{ approximately.}$$

This number R = 3438 is used even in the ancient Surya Siddhanta. For the information of the sine-table, Aryabhatta provides a rule which gives the values of R sines of 24 angles at equal intervals of 225 minutes or 3° 45' each. The rule says that "the R sine-differenes, (at intervals of 225 minutes of arc) in munites of arc are 225, 224, 222, 219, 215, 210, 205, 199, 191, 183, 174, 164, 154, 143, 131, 119, 106, 93, 79, 65, 51, 37, 22 and 7".

Thus the first value of Rsin (225') is equal to 225'. The successive values for the subsequent angles, at intervals of 3°45' are obtained by successively adding the R sine-differences given above; namely

224, 222, etc. We list below in the table the values compared with current values.

Table 5.3: R sines of angles

θ	Indian Jya (θ)	Current R sinθ	θ	Indian Jya(θ)	Current R sinθ
3° 45'	225	224.856	48° 45'	2585	2584.825
7° 30'	449	448.749	52° 30'	2728	2727.549
11° 15'	671	670.720	56° 15'	2859	2858.592
15° 0'	890	889.820	60° 0'	2978	2977.395
18° 45'	1105	1105.109	63° 45'	3084	3083.448
22° 30'	1315	1315.666	67° 30'	3177	3176.298
26° 15'	1520	1520.589	71° 15'	3256	3255.546
30° 0'	1719	1719.000	75° 0'	3321	3320.853
33° 45'	1910	1910.050	78° 45'	3372	3371.940
37° 30'	2093	2092.922	82° 30'	3409	3408.588
41° 15'	2267	2266.831	86° 15'	3431	3430.639
45° 0'	2431	2431.033	90° 0'	3438	3438.000

The problem of finding solutions in integers for x and y in an equation of the form $ax + c = by$, where a, b and c are given integers was given great importance by the ancient Indian mathematicians and astronomers. The subject of solving such indeterminate equations is known as Kuttaka method. Although such equations were solved even in Sulvasutras, the credit of providing a systematic method of solution goes to Aryabhatta. His commentators have explained the method elaborately which Aryabhatta gives in two stanzas. We shall return to this subject now known as Diophantine equations later.

Aryabhatta gives the formula for the area of a general triangle "the product of the perpendicular (from the vertex to the base) and half the base gives the measure of the area of the triangle." A theorem with proof, we find in Aryabhattiyam is the following:

Theorem: *If in a circle, a chord CD and diameter AB intersect each other at right angles at E, then $AE \cdot EB = CE^2$.*

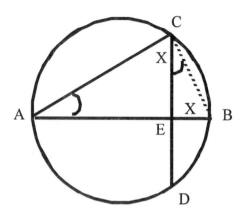

Figure 5.4: Area of a Triangle

Proof: In the triangles AEC and CEB, we have

$$\overset{\wedge}{CEA} = \overset{\wedge}{CEB} = 90°, \overset{\wedge}{CAE} = 90° - \overset{\wedge}{ACE} = \overset{\wedge}{ECB},$$

and
$$\overset{\wedge}{ACE} = 90° - \overset{\wedge}{ECB} = \overset{\wedge}{EBC},$$

so that triangles AEC, CEB are similar. Therefore,

$$\frac{AE}{CE} = \frac{CE}{EB} \text{ or } AE \cdot EB = CE^2. \qquad \text{Q.E.D.}$$

In the calculations of eclipses, some geometrical results are very important. Aryabhatta gives one such result as follows:

> If two circles intersect (at two points) and ACGBD be the line with the points in the given order, through the centers, then the "arrows" CG and BG of the intercepted arcs, in terms of the "erosion" BC are given by
>
> $$CG = \frac{(AB-BC)BC}{(AB+CD)-2BC} \text{ and } BG = \frac{(CD-BC)BC}{(AB+CD)-2BC}.$$

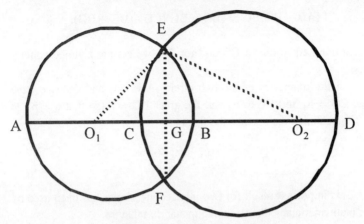

Figure 5.5: The Erosion of BC

Proof: In Figure 5.5, two circles with centers O_1 and O_2 and diameters d_1 and d_2 intersect at E and F. The portion BC, of the line ACGBD through O_1 and O_2 is called grasa and CG, BG are called sara or sampata sara ("arrows") of the two circles.

Since in the circle with O_1 as the center the chords AB and EF intersect at G, we see that

$$AG \cdot GB = EG \cdot GF.$$

Similarly, from the other circle with center O_2, we get

$$CG \cdot GD = EG \cdot GF.$$

From the foregoing relations, it follows that

$$AG \cdot GB = CG \cdot GD.$$

Expressing in terms of diameters, we obtain

$$(AB - BC + CG)(BC - CG) = CG(CD - CG),$$

and

$$(AB - BG)BG = (BC - BG)(CD - BC + BG).$$

Solving equation for CG and for BC, we get the claimed conclusions.

Let the diameters of the two circles $AB = d_1$ and $CD = d_2$, the Saras $CG = h_1$ and $BG = h_2$ and the grasa $BC = h$ (so that $h = h_1 + h_2$). The claimed results take the form

$$h_1 = \frac{(d_1-h)h}{(d_1+d_2)}, h_2 = \frac{(d_2-h)h}{(d_1+d_2)-2h}.$$

This important result for two intersecting circles has been used by later mathematicians like Brahmagupta and Mahavira.

We now give the results in progressions. An arithmetic progression is of the form $a, a + d, a + 2d, \ldots, a + (n - 1)d$. The sum S is given by $S = \frac{n}{2}[2a + (n - 1)d]$, and this was known before Aryabhatta. However, Aryabhatta provides the formula for the number of terms n as $n = \frac{1}{2d}\left[\sqrt{8dS + (2a - d)^2} - 2a + d\right]$. A couple of typical results given by Aryabhatta are $1^2 + 2^2 + 3^2 + \ldots + n^2 = \frac{1}{6}[n(n + 1)(2n + 1)]$, and $[1 + 2 + 3 + \ldots + n]^2 = \frac{1}{4}n^2(n + 1)^2$.

As we have seen, Bhaskara I is the greatest and the earliest exponent of Aryabhatta and his school of astronomy. Bhaskara I explains in Aryabhattiya Bhashyam extensively the too brief and aphoristic statements of Aryabhattiyam for the benefit of the readers. For example, Aryabhatta's brief statement of finding sine of an angle greater than 90°, is given more explicitly by Bhaskara I as follows:

$R \sin (90 + \theta) = R \sin 90 - R \text{ versin } \theta,$

$R \sin (180 + \theta) = R \sin 90 - R \text{ versin } 90 - R \sin \theta = - R \sin \theta,$

$R \sin (270 + \theta) = R \sin 90 - R \text{ versin } 90 - R \sin \theta + R \text{ versin } \theta$
$= - R \sin 90 + R \text{ versin } \theta,$

where $R \text{ versin } \theta = R(1 - \cos \theta)$, called Utkramajya($\theta$). Bhaskara I also explains clearly the method of securing the sine-table.

In his *Maha Bhaskariyam*, Bhaskara I has given an approximate formula for calculating R sine of an acute angle without using the table. His formula is

$$R \sin A = \frac{4R(180-A)A}{[40500-(180-A)A]}$$

where A is in degrees. If A is in radians, then formula takes the form

$$\sin A = \frac{16A(\pi-A)}{5\pi^2-4A(\pi-A)}.$$

For example, $\sin(\frac{\pi}{3}) = 0.8643\ldots$, $\sin(\frac{\pi}{7}) = 0.4313,\ldots$ and so on.

Bhaskara I offers the formula when the three sides of the triangle are given but not the altitude as,

$$\text{Area} = \sqrt{S(S-a)(S-b)(S-c)}$$

where $S = \frac{1}{2}(a+b+c)$, the semi-perimeter of the triangle, a, b, c being the three sides.

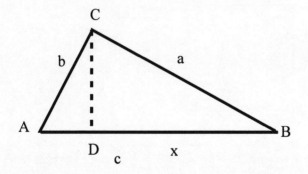

Figure 5.6: Area of a Triangle by Semi-Perimeter

Proof: Let $BD = x$ and AC, AB, and CB be denoted by b, c, and a. To find BD, we have

$$AC^2 = AD^2 + CD^2 = (AB - BD)^2 + CD^2$$

$$= AB^2 + (BD^2 + CD^2) - 2AB \cdot BD$$

$$= AB^2 + BC^2 - 2AB \cdot BD,$$

or equivalently, $b^2 = c^2 + a^2 - 2cBD$, which implies $BD = \frac{c^2+a^2-b^2}{2c} = x$. Now

$$CD = \sqrt{a^2 - x^2}$$

$$= \left[a^2 - \left(\frac{c^2+a^2-b^2}{2c} \right)^2 \right]^{\frac{1}{2}}$$

$$= \left[\frac{(2ac)^2 - (c^2+a^2-b^2)^2}{4c^2} \right]^{\frac{1}{2}}$$

$$= \left[\frac{(2ac+c^2+a^2-b^2)(2ac-c^2-a^2+b^2)}{4c^2} \right]^{\frac{1}{2}}$$

$$= \left[\frac{\{(c+a)^2-b^2\}\{b^2-(c-a)^2\}}{4c^2} \right]^{\frac{1}{2}}$$

$$= \left[\frac{(c+a+b)(c+a-b)(b+c-a)(b-c+a)}{4c^2} \right]^{\frac{1}{2}}$$

$$= \left[\frac{2S(2S-2b)(2S-2a)(2S-2c)}{4c^2} \right]^{\frac{1}{2}}$$

since, $c + a - b = 2S - 2b$ where $S = \frac{a+b+c}{2}$. We therefore have

$$CD = \frac{2}{c}[S(S-a)(S-b)(s-c)]^{\frac{1}{2}}.$$

Thus area of ABC $= \frac{1}{2}AB \cdot CD$

$$= \frac{1}{2}c \cdot \frac{2}{c}[S(S-a)(S-b)(S-c)]^{\frac{1}{2}}.$$

$$= \sqrt{S(S-a)(S-b)(S-c)}. \qquad \text{Q.E.D.}$$

Employing geometry to prove algebraic results, like identities, was the speciality of ancient Indian mathematicians. Here we give a typical result from Bhaskara I.

Problem: The two parallel faces of a figure resembling a drum-shaped musical instrument called Panava, are each 8 units, the central width 2 units, and the length between the faces is 16 units. Find the area of Panava.

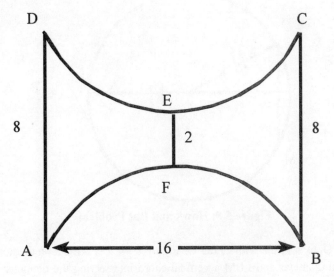

Figure 5.7: The Area of Panava

The figure AFBCED is Panava which is a combination of two identical trapeziums AFED and BFEC. Bhaskara I uses the formula

$$\text{Area} = \tfrac{1}{2}\left[\tfrac{AD+BC}{2} + EF\right]AB.$$

In the figure AD = BC = 8, EF = 2, AB = 16 and therefore

$$\text{Area} = \tfrac{1}{2}\left[\tfrac{8+8}{2} + 2\right]16 = 80 \text{ square units.}$$

We can find several interesting problems in Bhaskara I, such as hawk-and-rat and crane-and-fish; which are very interesting.

Let us start with the hawk and rat problem. A hawk is sitting on a pole whose height is 18 units. A rat which had gone out of its dwelling, at the foot of the pole, to a distance of 81 units, while returning to its dwelling, is killed by the hawk on the way. Find how far it has gone towards the hole and also the horizontal motion of the hawk (the speeds of the rat and the hawk being the same).

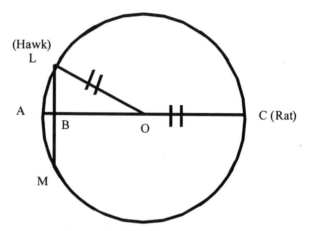

Figure 5.8: Hawk and Rat Problem

Draw a circle with center O (Figure 5.8). Let ABOC be the horizontal diameter and LBM a vertical chord intersecting the diameter at B. Now, BL is the pole and BC is the track of the rat. The hawk is perching at the top of the pole L and B is the hole, the abode of the rat. The rat has traversed 81 units to C. The hawk, sitting at L, sees the rat moving from C towards B and swoops down to attack it. The hawk catches the rat at O traversing a distance LO. Assuming that the hawk and the rat travel at the same speed, the time taken by the hawk to travel LO is the same as the time taken by the rat to travel CO and hence LO = CO.

We know that LB = 18 units and BC = 81 units. We have

$$LB \cdot BM = AB \cdot BC,$$

or $$LB^2 = AB \cdot (81),$$

so that AB = 4 units. Hence,

$$BO = \tfrac{1}{2}(BC - AB) = 38\tfrac{1}{2} \text{ units},$$

and $$CO = \tfrac{1}{2}(BC + AB) = 42\tfrac{1}{2} \text{ units}.$$

This means that the distance traversed by the rat is $42\tfrac{1}{2}$ units and the horizontal distance traversed (BO, projection of LO) is $38\tfrac{1}{2}$ units.

Next we shall discuss the crane and the fish problem. There is a reservoir of water of dimensions 6×12. At the north-east corner of the reservoir there is a fish; and at the north-west corner there is a crane. For the fear of the crane, the fish, crossing the reservoir, hurriedly went towards the south in an oblique direction but was killed by the crane who came along the sides of the reservoir. Give out the distances travelled by them, assuming their speeds are the same.

In Figure 5.9, LBQP is the reservoir in which BQ = LP = 12 and LB = PQ = 6. Let LB be on the eastern side, PQ on the west, LP the north and BQ the southern side of the reservoir. The fish is at L and the crane P. The fish swims towards the southern side of the reservoir and reaches a point O on BQ. In the same interval of time, the crane walks swiftly along the edges PQ and then QB and attacks the fish at O on the edge QB. Since the speeds are assumed to be the same, the fish and the crane travel equal distances in the same interval of time. Therefore, we get

$$LO = PQ + QO.$$

Extend OQ up to C such that OC = OL. Thus

$$BC = BQ + PQ = 12 + 6 = 18.$$

Let CB be extended intersect the circle at A. Then it follows that

$$AB \cdot BC = LB^2$$

so that

$$AB = LB^2/BC = 36/18 = 2.$$

Hence, $AC = AB + BC = 2 + 18 = 20$ so that $OC = AC/2 = 10$ and therefore $OL = OC = 10$. This means that the crane and the fist travel a distance of 10 units each.

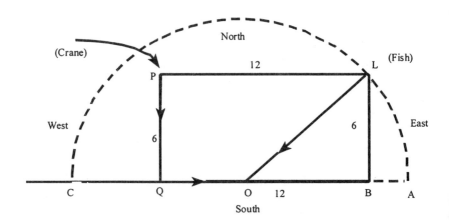

Figure 5.9 Crane-fish problem

Chapter 6

From Brahmagupta to Nilakanta

Brahmagupta (born in 30 B.C.) occupies an important place in the history of ancient Indian astronomy and mathematics. He maintained, for example, that "all things fall to the earth by a law of nature, for it is the nature of the earth to attract and keep things." Thus Newton's law of gravitation is anticipated by almost a millennium and a half. Sometime later, twenty scientists were invited to Baghdad who carried a collection of scientific works including Brahma Siddhanta of Brahmagupta. All of them were translated to Arabic. One of them called "Sind-Hind" in Arabic exercised an important influence on Arabic astronomy. References to Brahmagupta's works occur frequently in Arabic literature.

Brahmagupta concentrated on rational right-angled triangles and quadrilaterals. For example, his general solution for a rational right angled triangle ABC is

$$a = 2mn, b = m^2 - n^2 \text{ and } c = m^2 + n^2,$$

where m and n are unequal rational numbers. An interesting modification given is as follows: Suppose that a side "a" different from the hypotenuse is given. Then, for any rational number m, the sides of the rational right-angled triangle is given by

$$a, \frac{1}{2}[\frac{a^2}{m} - m] \text{ and } \frac{1}{2}[\frac{a^2}{m} + m].$$

Here is a typical theorem of Brahmagupta.

Theorem: *The rectangle contained by two sides of a triangle is equal to the rectangle contained by the circum-diameter and the altitude to the base.*

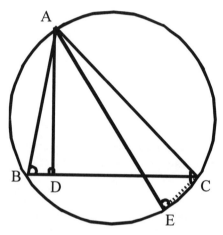

Figure 6.1: The Rational Right-Angled Triangle

Proof: In triangle ABC, AD is the altitude to the base BC and AE is the circum-diameter. Join CE.

In triangles ACE and ABD, $A\widehat{C}E = A\widehat{D}B = 90°$, (angle in a semi-circle being a right-angle) $A\widehat{E}C = A\widehat{B}D$ (i.e., $A\widehat{B}C$), (being angles standing on the same arc AC), and hence the remaining angles

$$C\widehat{A}E = D\widehat{A}B.$$

Hence, triangles ACE and ADB are similar and therefore

$$\frac{AC}{AE} = \frac{AD}{AB} \text{ or } AB \cdot AC = AD \cdot AE. \qquad \text{Q.E.D.}$$

There are several results on the area of cyclic quadrilaterals.

Brahmagupta states that the exact area of a cyclic quadrilateral is "the square root of the product of four factors which are half the sum of the sides (respectively) diminished by the sides." That is, if a, b, c and d are the sides of a cyclic quadrilateral ABCD and 2s is their sum, then

$$\text{Area of ABCD} = [(s-a)(s-b)(s-c)(s-d)]^{\frac{1}{2}}$$

where, of course, $2s = (a+b+c+d)$. This formula was rediscovered in Europe nearly a thousand years later by W. Snell in 1619 A.D.

The following is another theorem on the diagonals of a convex quadrilateral inscribed in a circle.

Theorem: *Divide mutually the sums of the products of the sides attached to both the diagonals and then multiply the quotients by the sum of the products of the opposite sides; the square-roots of the results are the diagonals of the quadrilateral.*

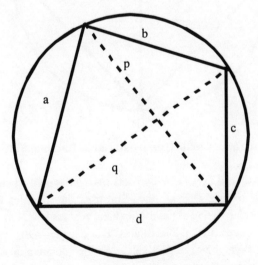

Figure 6.2: Diagonals of a Cyclic Quadrilateral

Let a, b, c and d be the four sides of a convex cyclic quadrilateral and p and q, the diagonals as shown in Figure 6.2. Then

$$p = \left[\frac{(ab+cd)(ac+bd)}{(ad+bd)} \right]^{\frac{1}{2}}, \quad q = \left[\frac{(ad+bc)(ac+bd)}{(ab+cd)} \right]^{\frac{1}{2}}.$$

The next result is concerned with cyclic quadrilaterals with rational sides.

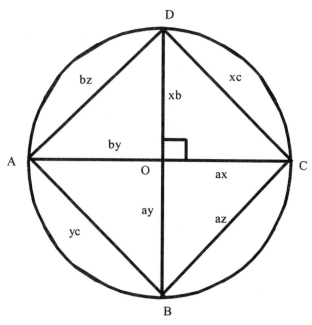

Figure 6.3: Cyclic Quadrilaterial of Rational Sides

Let (a,b,c) and (x,y,z) be two sets of right-angled triangles such that $c^2 = a^2 + b^2$ and $z^2 = x^2 + y^2$. Construct the triangles BOC and COD having sides (ax,ay,az) and (xa,xb,xc) respectively. On the other side of BD, construct the triangles DOA and AOB with sides (bx,by,bz) and (ya,yb,yc) respectively. We then obtain a quadrilaterial ABCD having the sides cy, az, cx and bz. The diagonals AC and BD are at right-angles.

It follows that the quadrilaterial ABCD is cyclic since the circum-radius of triangle ABD=$\frac{1}{2} \frac{bcyz}{by} = \frac{1}{2}cz$, and the circum-radius of triangle

ACD=$\frac{1}{2}\frac{caxz}{ax} = \frac{1}{2}cz$. Therefore, if S is the circum-center of the triangle ABD, the circle with S as the center and $\frac{1}{2}cz$ as the radius will pass through A, B, C and D.

As an example, take two rational right-angled triangles with sides (3, 4, 5) and (12, 5, 13). Then, following the method discussed above, the quadrilaterial with sides (39, 52, 60, 25) is a rational cyclic quadrilaterial in which the sides, the diagonals and even the area are rational. The circum-diameter of this cyclic quadrilaterial is 65, a rational number. This quadrilateral is referred to as *Brahmagupta's quadrilaterial* which has been identified in the west, in a slightly transformed form, diagonals being interchanged with a pair of opposite sides. In fact, this was the only rational cyclic quadrilaterial known to the western mathematicians till the time of Euler (1707-1783). The German mathematician, Kummer (1810-1893) in one of his papers shows that Brahmagupta's simple method gives all rational cyclic quadrilaterals.

The most remarkable contribution of Brahmagupta is the solution of the second order indeterminate equation in the form

$$Nx^2 + 1 = y^2,$$

where N is an integer. For a given integer N, the problem is to find values of x and y in integers. Before obtaining the solution, Brahmagupta establishes two results.

(1) Suppose that a solution of $Nx^2 + 1 = y^2$ is given, namely $x = \alpha$, and $y = \beta$. Then $x = \alpha\beta_1 \pm \alpha_1\beta$, $y = \beta\beta_1 \pm N\alpha\alpha_1$ is a solution of $Nx^2 \pm \kappa\kappa_1 = y^2$. This implies that if

$$N\alpha^2 \pm \kappa = \beta^2 \text{ and } N\alpha_1^2 \pm \kappa_1 = \beta_1^2,$$

then $\qquad N(\alpha\beta_1 \pm \alpha_1\beta)^2 + \kappa\kappa_1 = (\beta\beta_1 \pm N\alpha_1)^2.$

In particular, if $N\alpha^2 + \kappa = \beta^2$, then $N(2\alpha\beta)^2 + \kappa^2 = (\beta^2 + N\alpha^2)^2$. The above results are called "Bhavana." These are further categorized as "Samasa Bharvana" (addition lemma) and Antara Bhavana (subtraction lemma). It is clear from this result that when two solutions of $Nx^2 + 1 = y^2$ are known, any number of solutions can be obtained.

For, if (a,b) and (a_1, b_1) are two solutions, then $x = ab_1 \pm a_1 b$, $y = bb_1 \pm Naa_1$ are two other solutions. Also, if (a,b) is a solution, then $(2ab, b^2 + Na^2)$ is another solution. Hence by repeated application, it follows that the equation $Nx^2 + 1 = y^2$ has infinitely many solutions. To do this it is necessary to know one solution to start with.

If $x = \alpha$, $y = \beta$ is a solution of $Nx^2 + \kappa^2 = y^2$, then $x = \frac{\alpha}{\kappa}$, $y = \frac{\beta}{\kappa}$ is a solution of $Nx^2 + 1 = y^2$. This is another result which can be employed to find the solutions. For example, the solutions of

(i) $6x^2 + 12 = y^2$
(ii) $6x^2 + 75 = y^2$, and
(iii) $6x^2 + 300 = y^2$,

can be derived from the solutions of $6x^2 + 3 = y^2$ because,

(i) $12 = 2^2 \times 3$
(ii) $75 = 5^2 \times 3$ and
(iii) $300 = 10^2 \times 3$.

As we have seen, Brahmagupta's method needs a trial solution to solve the equation $Nx^2 + 1 = y^2$. We shall see later that Bharskarachaya's Chakravala method removes this handicap.

Note that, in the current literature, this equation $Nx^2 + 1 = y^2$ is known as Pell's equation after John Pell (1611-1685 A.D.) and it is stated that Fermat (1657 A.D.) was the first to assert that it has infinitely many integer solutions.

Brahmagupta also provides the second difference interpolation formula long before the rediscovery of Newton-Stirling formula in the form $f(x + nh) = f(x) + \frac{n}{2}[\Delta f(x - h) + \Delta f(x)] + \frac{n^2}{2}\Delta^2 f(x - h)$.

Bhaskaracharya is the most popular among the Indian mathematicians and astronomers. His popular text is known as *Leelavati* written in 486 A.D. Bhaskaracharya's greatness lies in making mathematics highly irresistable and attractive. He is generally referred to as Bhaskara II to distinguish him from Bhaskara I. Bhaskaracharya's celebrated work *Siddhanta Siromani* consists of four parts, namely, Leelavati, Bijaganitam, Grahaganitam and Goladhyaya. The first two exclusively deal with mathematics and the last two with astronomy.

We have seen that Brahmagupta has the unique honor of discovering the method to solve the equation of the form $Nx^2 + 1 = y^2$ by his "Bhavana" method. Bhaskara II improved Brahmagupta's method by his chakravala (cyclic) method. Bhaskara II dispenses with the prior knowledge of a trial solution to start. His method is essentially as follows:

$$Nx^2 + \kappa = y^2 \text{ when } \kappa = \pm 1, \pm 2 \text{ or } \pm 4.$$

Then one can find a and b such that $Na^2 + \kappa = b^2$ for any suitable κ. One also has $N \cdot 1^2 + (m^2 - N) = m^2$. Applying Samasa Bhavana, we obtain

$$N\left[\frac{am+b}{\kappa}\right]^2 + \frac{m^2-N}{\kappa} = \left[\frac{bm+Na}{\kappa}\right]^2. \tag{*}$$

To use the "Kuttaka" method of Bhaskara II, we choose m such that $am + b$ is divisible by κ, where m is suitably chosen so as to make $(m^2 - N)$ numerically small. We let

$$\frac{am+b}{\kappa} = a_1, \quad \frac{m^2-N}{\kappa} = \kappa_1 \text{ and } \frac{bm+Na}{\kappa} = b_1,$$

then we have the following theorem of Bhaskara II: If a_1 is an integer, then b_1 and κ are also integers. When a_1, b_1 and κ_1 are integers, equation (*) takes the form $Na_1^2 + \kappa_1 = b_1^2$. Now using a_1, b_1, κ_1 instead of a,b,κ, we repeat the process. Let the new set of integers thus generated be a_2, b_2, κ_2, so that $Na_2^2 + \kappa_2 = b_2^2$. One can repeat this process successively. We have then the next theorem of Bhaskara II: After a finite number of steps, two integers α and β can be obtained such that

$$N\alpha^2 + \lambda = \beta^2 \text{ where } \lambda = \pm 1, \pm 2 \text{ or } \pm 4.$$

Thus starting with $Na^2 + \kappa = b^2$, where κ is a convenient integer, one can get a solution α, β of the equation $Nx^2 + \lambda = y^2$, where λ takes the values $\pm 1, \pm 2$ or ± 4. Once this solution is obtained, Brahmagupta's technique will lead to an integral solution of the given equation $Nx^2 + 1 = y^2$.

As an example, consider the equation $61x^2 + 1 = y^2$. We have $61 \times 1^2 + 3 = 8^2$ so that $a = 1$, $\kappa=3$ and $b = 8$. Now choose m so that $\frac{am+b}{\kappa} = \frac{m+8}{3}$ is an integer and $\frac{m^2-N}{\kappa} = \frac{m^2-61}{3}$ is numerically small. Let $m = 7$ and we get

$$a_1 = \tfrac{am+b}{\kappa} = 5, \; \kappa_1 = \tfrac{m^2-N}{\kappa} = -4 \text{ and } b_1 = \tfrac{bm+Na}{\kappa} = 39.$$

Hence $61 \times 5^2 - 4 = 39^2$ which is of the form $Nx^2 + \lambda = y^2$. Since $\lambda = -4$, it means that $61(\tfrac{5}{2})^2 - 1 = (\tfrac{39}{2})^2$. Now by Samasa Bhavana between

$$1, 8, 3 \text{ and } \tfrac{5}{2}, \tfrac{39}{2}, -1, \text{ we have } \tfrac{195}{2}, \tfrac{1523}{2}, 1.$$

Next we perform Samasa between $\tfrac{195}{2}, \tfrac{1523}{2}, 1$ and $\tfrac{5}{2}, \tfrac{39}{2}, -1$, we find that $\alpha = 3805, \; \beta = 29718, \; \lambda = -1$. Finally, performing Samasa on this set itself, one obtains the solution

$$x = 226153980, \; y = 1766319049.$$

We note that these are the least integral values of x and y satisfying the equation $61x^2 + 1 = y^2$.

We learn that Fermat, in 1657 A.D., proposed this problem to Frenicle and other fellow mathematicians as a challenge and none succeeded in solving.

We shall next give some typical interesting problems from Leelavati.

Problem 1: A beautiful pearl necklace of a young youthful lady was torn in a love quarrel and the pearls were all scattered on the floor. One third of the number of pearls was on the bed, one-fifth was under the bed, one-sixth was found by the pretty lady, one-tenth was collected by the lover and six were seen hanging on the thread. Tell me the total number of pearls in the necklace.

If the number of pearls in the necklace is x, then the problem yields the equation

$$\tfrac{x}{3} + \tfrac{x}{5} + \tfrac{x}{6} + \tfrac{x}{10} + 6 = x.$$

Solving this we get x = 30.

Problem 2: The square-root of half of a swarm of bees went to a rose-bush to suck honey followed by eight-ninths of the entire swarm. One lady bee was caught in a lotus flower which closed at night. She was humming in response to the humming call of a male bee. O lady, tell me the number of bees in the swarm.

Solution: Let x be the total number of bees in the swarm. Then the number of bees which went to the rose-bush is $\sqrt{\frac{x}{2}} + \frac{8}{9}x$. Out of the remaining, the she-bee was caught in the lotus at night and was responding to the love-hum of the male bee. Including this couple bees in love, together with those in the rose-bush, we get the total number of bees x in the swarm. That is

$$\sqrt{\frac{x}{2}} + \frac{8}{9}x + 2 = x$$

so that

$$\sqrt{\frac{x}{2}} = x - \frac{8}{9}x - 2$$

or equivalently,

$$\sqrt{\frac{x}{2}} = \frac{x}{9}x - 2 = \frac{x-18}{9}.$$

Squaring both sides, we get

$$\frac{x}{2} = \frac{(x-18)^2}{81}$$

or $2(x - 18)^2 - 81x = 0$, which implies

$$2x^2 - 153x + 648 = 0, \text{ or } (x - 72)(2x - 9) = 0.$$

This gives x = 72 as the valid answer.

Problem 3: There are two bamboos of heights 15 and 10 feet standing on the ground and light strings are tied from the summit of either bamboo to the foot of the other. Find the perpendicular distance of the point of intersection of the two strings from the ground.

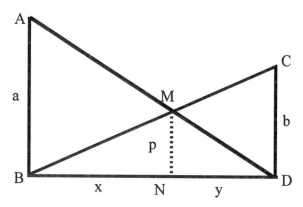

Figure 6.4: The Idea of Locus

Solution: Suppose that AB and CD are two vertical bamboos of heights a and b respectively. The two strings AD and BC intersect at M. The perpendicular distance of M from the ground is MN which is to be found. Let BN = x and ND = y and MN = p. Now the triangles MND and ABD are similar and therefore $\frac{ND}{BD} = \frac{MN}{AB}$ which yields $\frac{y}{x+y} = \frac{p}{a}$. Similarly, MNB and CDB are similar and hence, we have $\frac{x}{x+y} = \frac{p}{b}$. Consequently, $\frac{p}{a} + \frac{p}{b} = \frac{y}{x+y} + \frac{x}{x+y} = 1$ or equivalently, $p[\frac{a+b}{ab}] = 1$ and therefore $p = \frac{ab}{a+b}$ is the answer.

It is important to note that p does not depend on the distance between the bamboos.

Bhaskara II gives the solutions of a cubic and a biquadratic equations in his *Bijaganitam*.

Problem 4: Solve the cubic equation

$$x^3 + 12x = 6x^2 + 35.$$

Solution: The equation can be written as

$$x^3 - 6x^2 + 12x - 8 = 27,$$

or
$$(x-2)^3 = 3^3,$$
so that $x - 2 = 3$ or $x = 5$.

This is the only real root.

Problem 5: Solve the biquadratic equation

$$x^4 - 2x^2 - 400x = 9999.$$

Solution: Adding $4x^2 + 400x + 1$ to both sides, one gets

$$x^4 + 2x^2 + 1 = 4x^2 + 400x + 10,000,$$

or $(x^2 + 1)^2 = (2x + 100)^2$, which in turn gives $x^2 + 1 = 2x + 100$, that is, $x^2 - 2x + 1 = 100$, or $(x - 1)^2 = 100$, which yields $x = 11$.

Bhaskara also provides several trigonometric formulas including

$$\sin(x \pm y) = \frac{\sin x \cos y \pm \cos x \sin y}{R},$$

where x, y are in degrees. We shall now show how this formula led Bhaskara II to arrive at the differential formula

$$\delta(\sin x) = \cos x \cdot \delta x$$

as follows.

Since taking $y = 1$, we get $\sin(x + 1) = \frac{\sin x \cos 1 + \cos x \sin 1}{R}$, it follows

$$\sin(x + 1) = \sin x + \frac{\cos x \sin 1}{R} \text{ approximately,}$$

and therefore, we have

$$\sin(x + 1) - \sin x = \frac{\cos x \cdot 60}{R}.$$

Bhaskara II saw in the last equation that the increments in sines of his table of 90 sines are proportional to cos x. Let it be now required to find $\sin(x + \delta x)$ where δx is less that 60' and let $\frac{60 \cdot \cos x}{R} = y$ where y is called "Bhagyakhanda." Then Bhaskara argues that if for 60' of the argument, there is an increment of y in the sine, what will it be for δx?"

The result is $\frac{y\delta x}{60}$. But $y = \frac{60 \cos x}{R}$ and therefore

$$\frac{y\delta x}{60} = \frac{60 \cos x}{60 R}\delta x = \frac{\cos x \cdot \delta x}{R}.$$

Thus $\sin(x + \delta x) - \sin x = \frac{\cos x \cdot \delta x}{R}$, which means

$$\delta(\sin x) = \frac{\cos x \cdot \delta x}{R}$$

which corresponds to the modern formula $\delta(\sin x) = \cos x \cdot \delta x$.

Bhaskara also states that the derivative (taken as a ratio of differentials) vanishes at a maxima. He says "where the planet's motion is maximum, there the fruit of the motion is absent, that is stationary." Bhaskara introduces the concept of instantaneous motion in a planet in the chapter on true positions of planets of his *Siddhanta Siromani*.

Next comes Mahavira (815-878 A.D.) who wrote *Ganita-sara Sangraha*. It enjoyed a unique privilege as a text book in South India.

To find the cube of a natural number, Mahavira gives several methods. He gave importance to the topic permutations and combinations. The number of ways of selecting out of n objects at a time, without regard for the order of selection, is given by

$$n_{C_r} = \frac{n(n-1)(n-2)\ldots(n-r+1)}{1\cdot 2\cdot 3\cdot\ldots\cdot r}.$$

The credit of giving this formula goes to Mahavira, which is attributed to Herrejoni (1634 A.D.) by D.E. Smith in his *History of Mathematics* Vol. II, 1925. Ironically, Smith wrote a foreword to Mahavira's work edited by M. Rangachaya in 1912. Also, Mahavira explicitly mentions that a negative number cannot have a square root giving reasons. He did discuss in detail the method of solving simultaneous equations in two or three variables.

We have already noted that Gregory-Leibniz series for $\frac{\pi}{4}$ exist in Nilakanta's work *Tantra Sangraha* (1500 A.D.). In fact, he has several interesting series expansions for π. He also makes use of a result involving the differential of the inverse sine function, namely,

$$\delta[(\sin^{-1}(e \sin w)] = \frac{e \cos w}{\sqrt{1-e^2 \sin^2 w}} \partial w.$$

In his other book, *Aryabhattiya Bhashyam*, Nilakanta gives the formula

$$\Delta_2(\sin \theta) = -\sin \theta (2 \sin \tfrac{\Delta\theta}{2})^2,$$

which deals with the second difference of $\sin \theta$.

The credit of enunciating for the first time a formula for the sum of a (convergent) infinite geometric progression goes to Nilakanta. He explains the process of deriving the arc of a circle in terms of the chord by means of a computation which involves summing up of a convergent infinite geometric progression.

Nilakanta says, "Thus the sum of an infinite series, whose later terms (after the first) are obtained by diminishing the preceding one by the same divisor, is always equal to the first term divided by one less than the common mutual divisor."

This implies that if a is the first term and r is the common ratio, the geometric series is of the form

$$a + ar + ar^2 + ar^3 + \dots.$$

The sum of this infinite series, provided it is convergent (the condition is $-1 < r < 1$), is given by

$$S = \frac{a}{1-r}.$$

Example: Let $a = 1$ and $r = \tfrac{1}{2}$ so that the geometric series is

$$1 + \tfrac{1}{2} + \tfrac{1}{2^2} + \tfrac{1}{2^3} + \dots ,$$

and its sum is given by

$$S = \frac{1}{1-\tfrac{1}{2}} = 2.$$

Before Nilakanta was Ganesa Daivajna (979 A.D.) who wrote an astronomical treatise *Grahalaghava* and a commentary of *Siddhanta Siromani* of Bhaskara II. There are contributions to mathematics contained in the four famous Kerala works, namely, *Tantra Sangraha, Yuktibhasa, Karana Paddhati* and *Sadratnamala*, which were brought to light by C.M. Whish in 1835 A.D.

Chapter 7

Astronomical Aspects

What we did indicate so far in Chapters 5 and 6 is related to the origin of mathematics. All the mathematicians of ancient India, however, were astronomers and astronomical computations needed a significant amount of mathematics. For example, trigonometry (known as Trikonamiti) of planar as well as spherical was employed in astronomical work is clearly seen in Surya Siddhanta. The ancient tradition of India alludes to the existence of 18 Siddhantas (astronomical texts) out of which five are now known because the great astronomer Varahamihira in 123 B.C., codified the then existing five Siddhantas. Out of these five Siddhantas, Surya Siddhanta is popular and famous. By internal evidence, it was compiled when the present Kritayuga was still 1200 years to go, which computes to 2,166,302 years up to 2000 A.D. Surya Siddhanta also mentions that at the end of Kritayuga, in addition to the conjunction of seven planets at zero Aries, moon's apogee will be at 270 degrees in Capricorn, and moon's node at 180 degrees in Libra. Many commentaries of the original Surya Siddhanta were known and the presently existing edition of Surya Siddhanta must have undergone some changes because of the enormous time involved.

In 1860 A.D., Reverend E. Burgess published his translation of Surya Siddhanta. Depending on William Jones' arbitrary conclusion in 1774 A.D., that "the first ages of the Hindus were chiefly mythological and thus the historical age of India can not be carried further back to 2000 years before Christ," and the invented theory of Aryan invasion of India in the early 19th century, Burgess proclaims as follows,

> The old belief, under the influence of which Bailley could form his strange theories, namely, the belief in the immense antiquity of the Indian people and its immemorial possession of a highly developed civilization; the belief that India was the cradle of language, mythology, arts, sciences, and religion, has long since been proved an error. It is now well known that the Hindu culture cannot pretend to a remote origin than 2000 B.C.

Burgess was referring to the French astronomer Bailley, who verified the claims of ancient Indian astronomers and wrote "the Hindu systems of astronomy are by far the oldest, and from them the Egyptians, Greeks, Romans and even Jews derived their knowledge. The Indian tables give the same annual variation of the moon as that discovered by Tyco-Brahe, a variation unknown to the school of Alexandria, and also to the Arabs, who followed the calculations of this school."

Unfortunately for Burgess, nothing was proved as he claimed and therefore, he was totally in error.

Even stranger are the following absurd statements of Bently and Whitney. Bently, in his *Hindu Astronomy*, asserts that "the ancient astronomical literature of India is a mass of forgeries framed for the purpose of deceiving the world with respect to the antiquity of the Hindu people." Witness as well, Whitney's expressed opinion that "Hindus derived their astronomy and astrology from the Greeks and that what they did not borrow from the Greeks, they derived from other people, such as the Arabians, Chaldians and Chinese."

All the foregoing emotional haughty dismissals and refutations were accepted as proven facts and conclusions were drawn relative to ancient Indian astronomy and mathematics without any scholarly restraint. This prevailing view of distortions and conjectures still remains even though solid evidences are available to the contrary.

The representation of the celestial bodies and the various astronomical elements with the help of great and small circles in the celestial sphere necessitated handling of spherical triangles and their solutions. The properties of spherical triangles have been applied in connection with several astronomical problems. The following principal formulae for solving spherical triangles emerge from a series of astronomical rules scattered in astronomical texts such as Surya Siddhanta and its commentaries:

(i) $\cos a = \cos b \cos c + \sin b \sin c \cos A$;

(ii) $\cos A \sin c = \cos a \cos b - \sin a \cos b \cos C$;

(iii) $\frac{\sin a}{\sin A} = \frac{\sin b}{\sin B} = \frac{\sin c}{\sin C}$,

where A, B, C are the angles of a spherical triangle, of which opposite sides are a,b, c respectively. Let us consider the problem, as an illustration, of finding the rising times of different signs of the ecliptic on the equator above the horizon. This reduces to obtaining the relationship between the longitude λ (polar longitude in Indian astronomy), the obliquity σ and the declination δ of a planetary body on the ecliptic. The rule provided by Aryabhatta may be represented as

$$R \sin \delta = \frac{R \sin \lambda \cdot R \sin \sigma}{R}.$$

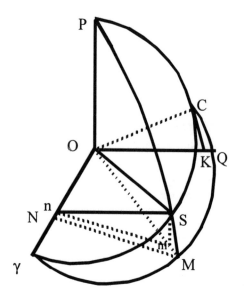

Figure 7.1: Solving Spherical Triangles

In Figure 7.1, γQ and γC are portions of the equator and the ecliptic, γ the first point of Aries, σ the obliquity, S the position of the planet, and CK, Sm and Sn are normals to OQ, OM and Oγ respectively. Then, from the properties of similar triangles, COK and Snm, $\frac{Sm}{Sn} = \frac{CK}{OC}$. Since $Sm = R \sin \delta$, $Sn = R \sin \lambda$, $CK = R \sin \sigma$ and $OC = R$, we get

$$R \sin \delta = \frac{R \sin \lambda \cdot R \sin \sigma}{R},$$

or equivalently,

$$\sin \delta = \sin \lambda \sin \sigma,$$

a relationship which follows directly from the spherical triangle γSM because of relation (iii).

In the treatment of the instantaneous motions of planets, Bhaskara II presents the idea of differentials. He defines two kinds of planetary velocities, the gross velocity (sthula gati) and the velocity at an instant of time (sukshma or tatkalika gati). In the former, change of longitude over a long interval of time is considered and the gross velocity is found by dividing the change in longitude by the interval of time. To find the tatkalika gati, it is necessary to find an infinitesimal change in longitude, $d\lambda$, corresponding to an infinitesimal time interval. Bhaskara II presents the following rule:

> To find the instantaneous velocity in longitude of the planet, the kotiphala is to be multiplied by the time rate of change of anomaly and divided by the radius, and the quotient thus obtained is to be added to or subtracted from the mean velocity of the planet according to its position in the six signs from the beginning of Cancer or Capricorn.

This rule can be expressed in mathematical notation as

$$\frac{d\lambda}{dt} = \frac{d\bar\lambda}{dt} \pm \frac{1}{R}(r\cos\alpha)\frac{d\alpha}{dt}, \tag{*}$$

where λ = true longitude, $\bar\lambda$ = mean longitude, α = anomaly, r = eccentricity or radius of the epicycle, $r\cos\alpha$ = kotiphala and R = radius of the different circle. According to the planetary theory, the equation of the center is given by

$$\sin\mu = \pm \frac{r\sin\alpha}{R}.$$

Since $\mu = \lambda - \bar\lambda$ is small, we get

$$\lambda - \bar\lambda = \pm \frac{r\sin\alpha}{R},$$

which leads to (*) on differentiation and using the result

$$\tfrac{\mathrm{d}}{\mathrm{dt}}(\sin t) = \tfrac{\cos t}{R},$$

that was proved in Chapter 6.

To find the area of a circle or the volume of a sphere consists in dividing the area or volume into a large number of small elements and then taking their sum. Bhaskara II had recourse to this method as we see from the exposition of Ganesa Daivajna, whose time is Sakakala 1429 which is equivalent to 979 A.D. In the case of a sphere, the entire volume is divided into a large number of pyramids of the same height equal to the radius of the sphere. The apex of each pyramid coincides with the center, and the base lies on the surface. The base of each pyramid is taken to be a unit of the scale by which the area of the surface of the sphere was reckoned. The volumes of those pyramids are then summed up to obtain the volume of the sphere. Clearly the idea of integration is imbedded here.

The existence of the expressions of infinite series for π, $\sin \theta$, $\cos \theta$ and $\tan \theta$ in Tantra Sangraha of Nilakanta (1500 A.D.) was brought to notice by C.M. Whish in 1835 A.D. They are as follows:

$$\tfrac{\pi}{4} = 1 - \tfrac{1}{3} + \tfrac{1}{5} - \tfrac{1}{7} + \tfrac{1}{9} - \ldots,$$

$$\sin \theta = \theta - \tfrac{\theta^3}{3!} + \tfrac{\theta^5}{5!} - \ldots,$$

$$\cos \theta = 1 - \tfrac{\theta^2}{2!} + \tfrac{\theta^4}{4!} - \ldots,$$

$$\theta = \tan \theta - \tfrac{1}{3}\tan^3\theta + \tfrac{1}{5}\tan^5\theta - \ldots.$$

Note that Gregory (1671 A.D.) and Euler (1739 A.D.) considered such infinite series much later.

In astronomical computations, the method of successive approximations, termed as Asakrit karma (repeated process) was very often employed by the ancient Indian astronomers and mathematicians. Many examples are given by Bhaskaracharya to demonstrate this method. For example, see verse 89, Triprasna in Siddhanta Siromani. The fame of ancient Indian astronomers spread westwards and their works were translated by the Arabs about 800 A.D. and then reached Europe. In fact, it is mentioned in the astronomical tables of Ben-Al-Adami, published in 920 A.D. that an Indian astronomer, well versed in that science, visited on invitation the court of the Khalif in eight century A.D., bringing with him several astronomical works. See also, Alberuni's *History of India*, original. According to Weber's catalogue, the earlier astronomical works, namely, Soma Siddhanta, Arya Siddhanta and Narada Siddhanta exist in the Berlin library. We also know a copy of Brahma Siddhanta was in possession of Bently.

According to Surya Siddhanta, in every Maha Yuga (in every 4,320,000 years) there are slight differences in the motions of heavenly bodies which make it necessary to correct the astronomical texts to suit the altered conditions. Varahamihira did not include the foregoing Siddhantas since they belonged to the earlier Maha Yugas. He only codified those Siddhantas which belong to the present Maha Yuga.

Chapter 8

Truth is Stranger than Fiction

New data challenging the controversial linear version of the human past have recently come from far and wide. Numerous discoveries of human remains and artifacts dating much earlier than 10,000 B.C. have been found. Moreover, there is a collection of evidence that the main stream archaeologists have rejected, namely, bones of anatomically modern humans in geological formations that are tens or even hundreds of millions of years old and signs of human presence in the Americas up to 750,000 years ago. Unfortunately, such evidence passes through a knowledge filter. Whatever evidence fits the paradigm is accepted even if it is flimsy, and whatever does not fit is suppressed no matter how solid it is.

If anatomically modern human beings have been on the Earth for millions of years and the natural cataclysms and catastrophes, in addition to human atrocities, have erased signs of whatever preceded, then it would be impossible to accurately reconstruct their history and civilization. Since the implications of finding a significant forgotten chapter in the human past would be immense, it is time for the pundits of various disciplines to unite to discover the nonlinear evolution process that would corroborate a very early period of the human past as described in the Vedic scriptures.

We learn from Rig Veda that

> Vedic people known as Bharatas and Aryans lived in three-story houses, built forts with iron and halls of Yajnas that had 1000 pillars and 100 doors, manufactured various types of weapons, crossed oceans in fast-moving ships for business and pleasure, constructed dams for rivers and used water from canals for agriculture, prepared medicines to keep people young and long-lived, had vehicles called Vimanas that flew in the air, were well-versed in astronomy and mathematics, and wore ornaments made with gold, diamonds and other precious stones.

This does not portend the static character of social structure of Vedic people of the East as is surmised. Moreover, the ancient people of the East did not use perishable material for preserving their knowledge either. For, Tala patras (palm leaves) were employed to write Vedic scriptures and other literature from time immemorial. The palm leaves were preserved by means of a special rasayana, a liquid prepared from certain plants that no longer is known. After palm leaves were immersed in this preservative, they were written upon with a metal pen and were then rendered indestructible. It is known that King Bhoja of seventh century A.D., found a great number of Nadi Sastras buried near the mountains which were preserved in this way.

We are told that since there are no primary sources which can give us a picture of the early development of Greek mathematics, we must rely on small fragments transmitted by later authors and scattered remarks by philosophers who were not mathematicians and therefore the prevailing account of the Greek mathematics in the formative years is largely hypothetical. The authentic history of Greece began with Phillipos of Macedon, the father of Alexander the Great and the period of Hellenism started after the death of Alexander in 323 B.C. Let us therefore summarize below, what we know about the ancient period of Greece from the work of the Greek historian Pococke.

Among the strongest peculiarities of the ancient heroic period of Greece, one knows the following. There was the perfection of arts,

abundance of gold, golden ornaments and vessels, the ample produce
of the loom, social refinement and comfort, constant use of war char-
iots, the art of metallurgy , the famous shield of Achilles, judicial in-
quiry, the musical festivities of marriages, and casting and carving both
in wood and metal. Also, one can trace in female dress, the magnifi-
cence of real wealth and simplicity of taste. There were earrings whose
pendant drops imitated the brilliance of the human eye. The robe was
fastened over the bosom with golden clasps, a fringe surrounded the
waist and completed the full dress costume of a lady of the Homeric
age. The whole of this state society, civil and military should strike
anyone as a carbon copy of the Vedic culture. The whole of Greece,
from the era of the supposed god-ships of Poseidon and Zeus, down to
the close of Trojan war was Vedic culture in language, sentiment and
religion as well as in arts of peace and war.

Considering the philosophy, poetry, history, and religion of the
Pelasgian colonists, they were not the savages feeding up on leaves and
acorns as was surmised, but were the chiefs of the Buddhistic faith of
North India who were driven beyond the Himalayan mountains carrying with them the germs of the European arts and sciences. We know
that Gautama Buddha lived during 1887-1807 B.C. and not during
563-483 B.C. as is usually assumed. This mighty human tide rolled towards its destined channel in Europe and in Asia to fulfill its beneficent
office in the moral fertilization of the world. The people of Buddhistic
faith immigrated to Bactria, Persia, Asia Minor, Greece, Phoenicia, and
Great Britain, carrying with them an astonishing degree of commercial
energy, skill in sciences of astronomy and mechanics. In the Greek
language alone there are ample evidences to substantiate this statement.
Greek language is a derivation from Sanskrit, disfigured from the
secondhand reception from the Greeks.

Pelasa, the ancient name of Bihar province in India and Pelaska is
a derivative from Pelasa, and the Greek "Pelasgoes" comes from
Pelaska. This was the strong hold of Buddhist faith. The "Maghedan"
are the people of Magadha, another name of the province of Bihar,
which comes from the Sage Magha. At the time of Maha Bharata, this
area was called Sisida. Because of numerous viharas or Biharas
(monasteries), it was called Bihar. The form "Makedonia" represents

the people of "Maghed'ha". The Pelasgians firmly settled in Greece at a period prior to the current historical knowledge of Greece.

According to Asius, one of the early poets of Greece (700 B.C.), King Pelasgus, the ancestor of the Pelasgi, sprang from the black earth. It is Gaya, the sacred city of Pelasa, that brought forth king Pelasgus, and not Gaia, the earth. This is history in Sanskrit but fable in Greek. Again, Aeschylus makes King Pelasgus, the son of Palaecthon. This certainly was true, since he was not son of Pale-thon or old land of Greek, but was a son of Palicthon, the land of Pali, so-called from the Pali, the language of Pelasa, Magadha or Bihar.

The same ignorance of primitive Grecian society, that marked the writers from Homer downwards, is seen in the treatment and etymological manufacture of the Cyclops. The Greeks first misunderstood the Pelasgic term and then fitted out a tale upon their own translation of what they imagined to be Greek, to imply that a Cyclope had a circular-eye in the middle of his huge forehead, a kind of monster. For Homer, Cyclopes were a race of shepherds, lawless, stern and gigantic. They were builders, archers and miners. They were skillful architects, as a Thracian tribe. From Thrace, they went to Crete and built mighty walls of Argos, Mycenae and Tiryns. Such walls are commonly known as Cyclopean walls, which still exist in various parts of ancient Greece and Italy. When these walls were built, the Greek Homer was not in existence, the language of Pelasa was still the principal medium of oral communication in Greece. The term "Cyclopes" is a corrupt form of "Goclopes", the people of Gocla country. The part of the country which was colonized by the Guc'lapes of the Jamuna river, was the Gucla-Des by the Greeks, written Cucla-Des by the English cyclades, that is, "the land of the Guc'las".

Who can imagine from the present barren land of Afghanistan, the elegant, the refined and the witty Athenian should have set out and yet it was so. The Attac, at present a small town on the east bank of the Indus river, gave a name to the far-famed province Attica. Philippos of Macedon was Bhili-pos or Bhil-prince. His son Alexander claimed descent from Hammon. He was correct, because "Hammon" lies between latitude 30 and 32 degrees and longitude 61 and 62 degrees, which is in present-day Afghanistan.

We learn that Pythagoras, who was born as far as we know in 580 B.C., was the founder of a brotherhood, originally brought together by religious influence. The son of an opulent merchant, Pythagoras traveled for thirty years and visited the Arabians, the Syrians, the Phoenicians, the Chaldeans, the Indians and the Gallic Druids. Pythagoras was a man of extensive research and acquired instruction but artful for mischief and destitute for sound judgement, is all that we know about him from his contemporaries. We are told that seeing a dog beaten, and hearing him howl, Pythagoras, desired the striker to desist, saying "It is the soul of a friend of mine, whom I recognized by his voice". The success of Pythagoras, as a person favored by the gods, and patentee of divine secrets, was very great. He had a select body of 300 adherents, most of them wealthy. His influence was over the populous city of Croton, much of Italy and Sicily. Pythagoras brought the doctrine of transmigration into Greece. His institutions are described as very monastic in their character, resembling closely the Viharas of Buddhists in India. His doctrines were widely spread over Greece, Italy, and Asia Minor for centuries after his death. Pythagoras, who taught Buddhist philosophy was a great missionary, whose name indicates his office and position when we realize that Pytha-goras in English is equivalent to Putha-goras in Greek and Budha-Guru in Sanskrit, which implies Buddhist's spiritual teacher.

As we have noted, the period of Hellenism began with the conquests of Alexander the Great. The whole near East had fallen to the Greeks when Alexander died in 323 B.C. Ptolemy, Alexander's childhood friend, returned Alexander's body to Egypt, where he established a Greek dynasty, that ended with Cleopatra. Ptolemy made a great effort to build a large library in Alexandria by bringing all knowledge together. Drawn like magnets, scholars descended on Alexandria from Europe and Middle East to study the secrets of earlier civilizations. Euclid (300 B.C.) studied at this marvelous library of Alexandria. Even Archimedes (287-212 B.C.) spent day after day unraveling the ancient scrolls.

Asrama schools and universities existed in Bharata Varsha to teach in the traditional manner. The well known universities were Takshasila, Nalanda, Nagarjuna, Vikramasila, Vallabhi, and Tamraparni to name a few. Nalanda clearly stood first because we know much about it from available information from the copper plate grant of Samudragupta (320-269 B.C.) and the Chinese scholar Yuan Chwang's testimony. We learn from Chinese scholar that by the middle of the seventh century A.D. Nalanda University was internationally famous. Nalanda had a wonderful library consisting of three buildings. Its standards were extremely high. The curriculum consisted of Vedic literature, philosophy, grammar, medicine, mathematics, and current literary works. Remember that in the whole of Europe, there were no universities until the Universities of Paris, Bologna and Oxford were founded in the twelfth century A.D.

Darkness and night descended on all the great centers of learning in India when the untutored Muslims poured into India with fire and swords at the beginning of the eleventh century A.D. Their first act was to raze the schools and universities, which in their eyes savored idolatrous worship. Nalanda was burned down. All the residents were put to death and the smoke from the burning manuscripts hung for days like a dark pale over the low Nalanda hills. A Muslim account of the destruction of Vikramasila University in 1203 A.D., for example, reveals that the entire collection of books was burnt and the inhabitants put to death under the impression that they were hated Brahmins.

Followed by Islamic invasions, appeared the racial and religious oppression of the Portuguese and the British Colonial rule. Christian missionaries of all denominations were united in their endeavor to destroy ancient scriptures in India. Every manuscript, every Sanskrit work that fell into the hands was immediately condemned and consigned to flames. Every new arrival received a formal order to dispose of all that might fall into their hands.

Nonetheless there exist several translations of original Sanskrit texts including Vedas, Puranas and Itihasas. Although European intellectuals like Schopenhauer, Voltaire, Goethe and Hegel admired the Sanskrit classics in the late 18th century, 19th century pundits dismissed the classics as fabrications. The translations are the writings of the biased Western scholars whose motivation was mainly political and religious, and stemmed from the belief that no one can excel the ancient Greeks. For example, the texts of the most puranas in their currently accepted editions are full of mistakes, distortions and inconsistencies. This is because of arbitrary selections, interpretations, interpolations, and alterations of manuscript copies, by the scholars to support their preconceived and fanciful theories.

After the Indian revolt in 1857, Thomas Macaulay established a network of English schools in India, with the goal of creating a new breed of Anglo-Indians who were "Indian in blood and color but English in taste, in morals, and in intellect." The plan was to turn the strength of Brahmins against them by utilizing their commitment to scholarship to uproot their own tradition. This plan succeeded so well that even today the same educational system prevails.

Thanks to the Vedic system, many families kept a set of ancient manuscripts. Therefore, in spite of all the destruction, we still possess a small portion of Vedic scriptures and these are good enough to rectify the prevailing theories.

Let us now sum up the facts.

1. There has been continuity of tradition in mathematics in ancient India from 3102 B.C.

2. There are mathematical texts in existence which positively date back to the pre-Christian Era. In fact, they go three thousand years before Christian Era.

3. There are certainly proofs in all ancient mathematical texts including Sulvasutras which are not even mathematical texts but only sacred books on alter constructions. The statements of Western scholars that only prescriptions of certain rules exist in them are completely false.

4. The theorem of Pythagoras and its converse was known in Sulvasutra period.

5. Trigonometry exists even in Surya Siddhanta which, as we have seen, is very very ancient.

6. Solving indeterminate equations was known to Sulvasutras. Aryabhatta gives the solution of first degree indeterminate equation. Brahmagupta solves the second order indeterminate equation of the form $Nx^2 + 1 = y^2$.

7. The contribution to the domain what we now call differential calculus was known positively to Bhaskara II in 486 A.D., long before Newton and Leibnitz. Of course, theorems on areas of plane figures and volumes of solid bodies were

known even before, which is the contribution to integral calculus.

8. The Greeks themselves had supposed that they had received their intellectual capital, especially in geometry, from the more ancient East.

9. The origin of mathematics is ancient India known as Bharata Varsha.

Well, truth is always stranger than fiction.

Notes and Comments

Chapter 1

It is important to remember that the Greek dates are obtained largely from the references of ancients to her predecessors and contemporaries, whereas Sanskrit chronology is of a literary historical kind coupled with astronomical verifications. Moreover, there are no primary sources which can give us a picture of the early development of Greek mathematics. One must rely on small fragments transmitted by later authors and scattered remarks in nonmathematical works. Hence what is reported is a largely hypothetical picture of Greek mathematics.

A seventh century Syrian Christian monk annoyed with Greek presumptions of complete superiority in the field of science, wrote a spirited defense of Syrian scientific knowledge and referred incidentally to India in these words, "I shall omit all discussions of the science of the Hindus, their subtle discoveries of the science of astronomy, discoveries that are more ingenious than those of Greeks and Babylonians and their computing that surpasses description. I wish only to say that this computation is done by means of nine signs."

The contents of Chapter 1 are adapted from [43] Stuik's book in a compact form. See also Ball [4], Bell [5] and Lakshmikantham [20].

Chapter 2

Sir Charles Elliot observed "scant justice is done to India's position in the world by these European histories which recount the exploits of her invader and leave the impression that her own people were a feeble, dreamy folk, sundered from the rest of mankind by their seas and mountain frontiers. Such a picture takes no account of the intellectual conquests of the Hindus." It is true, in particular, that significant accomplishments of ancient Indian astronomers and mathematicians has faded into insignificance. The constant indifference of scholars to the truth that the Greeks were not the inventors of geometry but Indians, is clearly unscholarly indeed.

Chapter 2 summarizes the developments based on the papers of Seidenberg [35, 36]. See also the related material in Ball [4], Burk [8], Cantor [9-11], Datta [15], Mahoney [22], Neugebauer [23-25], Renou and Felliozat [31], Seidenberg [34, 35], Sen and Bag [38], Thibaut [47, 48], Unguru [49] and Van der Warden [50, 51].

Chapter 3

One should remember that had there not been things of great importance in India, the Westerners would not have tried several voyages to reach India, the land of culture, riches and glory.

The Western scholars enjoyed the advantage of the prestige of the ruling class and the patronage of the government. They could therefore brush aside the protests of the independent Indian as well as European scholars and incorporate their fanciful theories into the textbooks which were prescribed for schools and universities.

The material of Chapter 3 is based on several sources. For further details, see Apte [2], Chandrasekhara Sastri [12], Feuerstein, Kak and Frawley [18], Frawley [19], Lakshmikantham [20], Rajaram [27], Ranga Charya [30], Sethna [39, 40], Talageri [45] and Venkatachalam [52-54].

Chapter 4

It is commonly believed that Islamic Arabia transmitted scientific knowledge of ancient India to Europe, which is a gross error. Early Islamic Arabia was not ready to learn anything from anybody, since its maxim was that everything worth learning was in the Koran. During the pre-Islamic time when Arabia was part of the worldwide Vedic culture, Europeans used to learn necessary knowledge from Arabian academics, because Christian onslaught had destroyed all the schools and academics in Europe. Hence European public who wish to learn anything had no other alternative but to flock to nearby centers in Arabia, Iran and Turkey, where Vedic schools and academics flourished until a rampant Islam blew out the torch of learning from west Asia too, following the example of Christian vandalism in Europe.

The brief narration of certain relevant chronological aspects given in Chapter 4 are taken from Lakshmikantham [20], Ranga Charya [30], Sethna [39, 40] and Venkatachalam [52-54].

Chapters 5 and 6

The mathematical ideas contained in Sulvasutras namely, Baudhayana, Apastamba and Katyayana Sulvasutras, are not their original. These results exist and are taught in Samhitas and Brahmanas and both are before Sulvaustras. Thus geometric algebra existed in ancient India long before the classical period in Greece. In this connection, it would be important to note that even the pottery of Vedic India made use of geometric patterns abundantly. For example, the Harappan culture made extensive use of repetition patterns that can be repeated indefinitely in any direction including circle, semicircles, triangles, hatched triangles, crosses and swastikas. Also, the so-called Pascal triangle, namely a triangular table of the coefficients of the expansion of $(a + b)^n$ was known as Mount Meru to Pingala before 200 B.C.

Indian numerals, commonly mislabeled as Arabic, were introduced by Indian merchants into Alexandria. Asoka Maurya used written numerals in his Brahmi inscriptions in 15th century B.C. and Aryabhatta (2765 B.C.) employed in his work, the zero, the decimals and the place value system. The concept of zero and the decimal system existed from Vedic times. The civilized world takes this ingenious numerical system for granted and forgets complacently what it owes to Vedic culture.

For the contents of mathematical results described in Chapters 5 and 6, see Balachandra Rao [3], Colebrooke [13], Dvivedi [16], Lakshmikantham and Vatsala [21], Rama Krishna Bhatt [28], Ranga Charya [29], Somayaji [32], Sarma [33], Shankara Shukla [41], Sreenivasa Ayyangar [42], Swarup Sharma [44] and Thibaut and Dvivedi [46].

Chapter 7

The material covered in Chapter 7 concerning astronomical aspects and related mathematical works is taken from Apte [1], Bose, Sen and Subbarayappa [6], Burgess [7], Somayaji [32] and Sarma [33].

Chapter 8

Just as today, we find true humans coexisting with various categories of apes, some more human than others, the same was true in the past, as far back as our search can carry us. In fact, an objective review of the evidence yields of anatomically modern human beings tens of millions of years ago, a fact distinctly incompatible with any current linear evolutionary models. From Vedic literature, we derive that the human race is of great antiquity.

Besides Alexandrians, colonies of other strangers found their way to South India, as refugees or traders in the early part of the Christian Era. Jews and Syrian Christians, escaping from the Roman persecution, both arrived in the first century B.C. As far back as history can probe, there has been no time when South India was not in contact with a number of foreign lands.

The contents of Chapter 8 are selected from Cremo and Thompson [14], Emerson Sen [17], Feuerstein, Kak and Frawley [18], Lakshmikantham [20], Pococke [26], Sethna [39, 40], Somayaji [32] and Venkatachalam [52-54].

References

[1] Apte, D.V. (editor), Daivajna, G. (author), *Tithi Chintamani*, Poona 1942.

[2] Apte, S., *Aryans: Who are they?*, Bharatiya Itihasa Sankalana Samiti, Mysore 1991.

[3] Balachandra Rao, S., *Indian Mathematics and Astronomy*, Jnana Deep Publications, Bangalore 1994.

[4] Ball, W.W.R., *A Short Account of the History of Mathematics*, (3rd Edition), London 1901.

[5] Bell, E.T., *Development of Mathematics*, New York 1940.

[6] Bose, D.M., Sen, S.N. and Subbarayappa, B.V., *A Concise History of Science in India*, Indian National Science Academy, New Delhi 1971.

[7] Burgess, Rev. E., *Surya Siddhanta* (Translation), Reprinted from the first edition of 1860 by Indological Book House, Delhi 1977.

[8] Burk, A., Das apastamba Sulvasutra, *Zeit. d. deutschen morgenlandischen Ges.* **55** (1901), **56** (1902).

[9] Cantor, M., Grake-indische studien, *Zeit. f. Math. u. Phys.***22** (1877).

[10] Cantor, M., Uber die alteste indische Mathematik, *Archive der Math. u. Phys.***8** (1904).

[11] Cantor, M., *Vorlesungen uber Geschichte der Mathematik*, Vol. **1**, Leipzig 1907.

[12] Chandrasekhara Sastri, *The Vedas,* Bharatiya Vidya Bhavan, Bombay 1993.

[13] Colebrooke, H.T. (editor), Chandra Banerjee, H. (translator), Bhaskaracharya (author), *Lilavati,* Calcutta 1927.

[14] Cremo, M. and Thompson, R., *Forbidden Archeology,* Bhakti Vedanta Institute, San Diego 1993.

[15] Datta, B., *The Science of the Sulva,* Calcutta 1932.

[16] Dvivedi, S. (editor), Bhaskaracharya, *Siddhanta Siromani,* Kashi Sanskrit Series, Benaras 1929.

[17] Emerson Sen, G., *The Pageant of Indian History,* David McKay Co., New York 1948.

[18] Feuerstein, G., Kak, S., and Frawley, D., *In Search of the Cradle of Civilization,* Quest Books, Wheaton, IL 1955.

[19] Frawley, D., *The Myth of the Aryan Invasion of India,* Voice of India, New Delhi 1994.

[20] Lakshmikantham, V., *The Origin of Human Past (Children of Immortal Bliss),* to appear.

[21] Lakshmikantham, V. and Vatsala, A.S., The origin of mathematics, *Nonlinear Studies* **5** (1998), 255-257.

[22] Mahoney, M.S., Babilonian algebra: Form vs. content, *Studies in History and Philosophy of Science* **1** (1971).

[23] Neugebauer, O., Mathematische Keilschrift-Texte, *Quellen u. Studien zur Geschichte d. Math Ast. u. Phys. Abt A*. **3** (1935).

[24] Neugebauer, O., *The Exact Sciences of Antiquity,* (2nd edition), New York 1962.

[25] Neugebauer, O., *Zur Geschichte der Pythagoraischen Lehrsatzes,* Nachrichten von der Gesellschaft der Wissenschaft zu Gottingen (Math. Phys. Klasse) 1928.

[26] Pococke, E., *India in Greece,* John J. Griffith and Co., Glasgow 1852.

[27] Rajaram, N.S., and Frawley, D., *Vedic Aryans and the Origins of Civilization,* W.H. Press, Quebec 1995.

[28] Ramakrishna Bhatt, M. (translator), Varahamihira (author), *Brihat Samhita,* Motilal Banarasidas, Delhi 1981

[29] Ranga Charya, M (editor and translator), Mahavira (author), *Ganita Sara Sangraha,* Madras 1912.

[30] Ranga Charya, V., *Pre-Historic India,* Vol. I 1937.

[31] Renou, L. and Felliozat, *J., L'Inde Classique I*, Paris 1947.

[32] Somayaji, D.A., *A Critical Study of the Ancient Hindu Astronomy*, Karnataka University, Dharwar 1971.

[33] Sarma, K.V. (editor), Somayaji, Nilakanta (author), *Tantra Sangraha*, V.V.B.I.S. & I.S., Hoshiarpur 1977.

[34] Seidenberg, A., Did Euclid's elements, Book 1, develop geometry axiomatically, *Archive for History of Exact Sciences* **14** (1975)

[35] Seidenberg, A., On the area of a semi-circle, *Archive for History of Exact Sciences* **1** (1962),

[36] Seidenberg, A., The origin of mathematics, *Archive for History of Exact Sciences*, **18** (1978), 301-342.

[37] Seidenberg, A., The ritual origin of geometry, *Archive for History of Exact Sciences* **1** (1962), 488-527.

[38] Sen, S.N. and Bag, A.K., *Sulvasutras of Baudhayana, Apastamba and Katyayana*, I.N.S.A., New Delhi 1983.

[39] Sethna, K.D., *Ancient India in a New Light*, Aditya Prakasan, New Delhi 1989.

[40] Sethna, K.D., *The Problem of Aryan Origins*, Aditya Prakasan, New Delhi 1992.

[41] Shankar Shukla, K. (editor and translator), Bhaskara I (author), *Mahabhaskariyam*, Lucknow 1960.

[42] Srinivasa Ayyangar, C.N., *The History of Ancient Indian Mathematics*, World Press Private Ltd., Calcutta 1967.

[43] Struik, D.J., *A Concise History of Mathematics*, (3rd edition), Dover Publications, New York 1967.

[44] Swarup Sharma, R. (editor and translator), Brahmagupta (author), *Brahmasphuta Siddhanta*, Indian Institute of Astronomical and Sanskrit Research, New Delhi 1981

[45] Talageri, S..G., *The Aryan Invasion Theory, A Reappraisal*, Aditya Prakasan, New Delhi 1993.

[46] Thibaut, G. and Dvivedi, S. (editors and translators), Varahamihira (author), *Pancha Siddhanta*, Motilal Banarasidas, Delhi 1930.

[47] Thibaut, G., On the Sulvasutras, *J. Asiatic Soc., Bengal* **9** (1874).

[48] Thibaut, G., Sulvasutras of Baudhayana, *The Pandit* **9** (1874) and **10** (1875), m.s.**1** (1876-1877).

[49] Unguru, S., On the need to rewrite the history of Greek mathematics, *Archive for History of Exact Sciences* **15** (1975).

[50] Van der Warden, B.L., Defense of a shocking point of view, *Archive for History of Exact Sciences* **15** (1976)

[51] Van der Warden, B.L., *Science Awakening* (2nd edition), Groningen 1961.

[52] Venkatachalam, K., *Bharatiya Sakamulu* (Telugu), Arya Vijnana Publications, Vijayawada 1950.

[53] Venkatachalam, K., *The History of Vikramaditya and Salivahana* (Telugu), Arya Vijnana Publications, Vijayawada 1951.

[54] Venkatachalam, K., *The Plot in Indian Chronology*, Arya Vijnana Publications, Vijayawada 1953.

Index

Author Biographical Sketches

Dr. V. Lakshmikantham

Dr. V. Lakshmikantham is an internationally well-known professor of mathematics at the Florida Institute of Technology in Melbourne, Florida USA. He is recognized as an authority, as well as the founder and developer of many research areas, of the broad scientific field of nonlinear analysis. He is responsible, as a researcher, for initiating, publicizing and popularizing several areas of nonlinear analysis as is evidenced by his numerous books.

As a scientific citizen, Lakshmikantham is virtually unsurpassed with an exceptional vision of the future. He founded the Journal of Nonlinear Analysis in 1976, established the International Federation of Nonlinear Analysis (IFNA) in 1991 and organized the first World Congress of Nonlinear Analysts (WCNA) in 1992 held in Tampa, Florida. The aim of the journal, the federation, and the congress is to have a forum on a global basis to forge unity in diversity, and for bringing more cooperation and collaboration into the world community at large. Lakshmikantham is totally responsible for keeping the society, IFNA viable and vital to nonlinear analysts around the world and almost single handedly organizing the World Congress of Nonlinear Analysts every four years.

He is the editor of five mathematical journals and the serves as a member on several editorial boards for various international journals. He has authored 30 research monographs and has published over 350 research papers in mathematics in the general area of nonlinear analysis. With all his research activity, teaching obligations, and administrative demands, he still found time to conduct research and publish, *The Origin of the Human Past* and write this monograph.

Dr. S. Leela

Dr. S.G. Leela is the Distinguished Professor of Mathematics at the State University of New York at Geneseo campus. She is the author of over 80 research papers and six research monographs in the areas of differential equations and nonlinear analysis. She has visited several countries giving invited lectures. She is an expert in the general area of nonlinear analysis and applications. She is a member of the editorial board of *Nonlinear Analysis* and *Mathematical Inequalities and Applications*.

Dr. Leela is a member of the American Mathematical Association (AMS), the Mathematics Association of America (MAA), SIAM, and the International Federation of Nonlinear Analysts (IFNA).

She received her B.Sc. (1955) and M.Sc. (1957) degrees from Osmania University, Hyderabad, India and her Ph.D. (1966) degree from Marathwada University, Aurangabad, India.

In addition to mathematics, she is interested in the Origin of Human Past as well as the Origin of Mathematics.